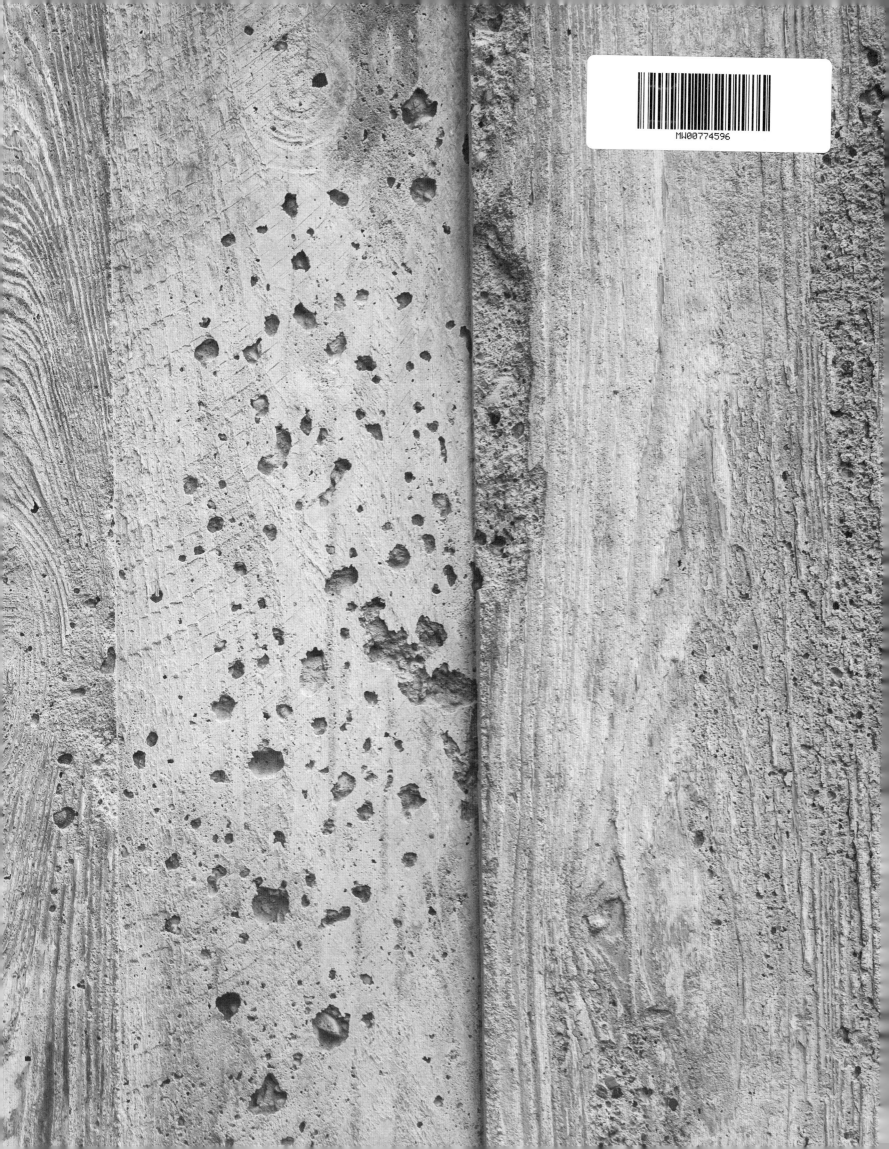

RUSTIC MODERN

RUSTIC MODERN

CHASE REYNOLDS EWALD   PHOTOGRAPHS BY AUDREY HALL

GIBBS SMITH
TO ENRICH AND INSPIRE HUMAN

Dedicated to the memory of Larry Andren, 1941–2017,
and to other similarly thoughtful architects
who pursue their calling with quiet integrity,
who lead by example and who, in respecting the land,
create iconic designs that leave a lasting legacy.

First Edition
25 24 23 22   10 9 8 7 6

Text © 2017 by Chase Reynolds Ewald
Photographs © 2017 by Audrey Hall

Published by
Gibbs Smith
P.O. Box 667
Layton, Utah 84041

1.800.835.4993 orders
www.gibbs-smith.com

Designed by Debbie Berne
Printed and bound in China

Gibbs Smith books are printed on either recycled, 100% post-consumer waste, FSC-certified papers or on paper produced from sustainable PEFC-certified forest/controlled wood source. Learn more at www.pefc.org.

Library of Congress Cataloging-in-Publication Data
Names: Ewald, Chase Reynolds, 1963- author.
Title: Rustic modern / Chase Reynolds Ewald ; photographs by Audrey Hall.
Description: First edition. | Layton, Utah : Gibbs Smith, 2017.
Identifiers: LCCN 2017000282 | ISBN 9781423644941 (jacketless hardcover)
Subjects: LCSH: Interior decoration--West (U.S.) | Decoration and ornament, Rustic--West (U.S.)
Classification: LCC NK2008 .E977 2017 | DDC 747.0978--dc23
LC record available at https://lccn.loc.gov/2017000282ISBN: 978-1-4236-4494-1

CONTENTS

INTRODUCTION

Rustic design begins—always—with the land. It is a response to it, it is an expression inspired by it, and it blends, practically and aesthetically, into its environment. Modern design seeks to express a current vision, a contemporary aesthetic. It shuns tradition for its own sake, avoiding nostalgic nods to the past, and it often stands out. In its energy, it conveys a certain optimism.

The new rustic modern design movement represents a harmonious and incredibly livable merging of two seemingly contradictory aesthetics. And it does so in a way that honors local tradition, regional vernacular, and sanctity of place while finding a fresh means of expression that looks to the future.

At its core, rustic modern is a response to the natural environment. It echoes organic materials and forms, and it is in constant dialogue with its surroundings. Fundamentally its modernist leanings are characterized by a metaphorical opening up displayed in lighter, cleaner, brighter interiors and,

crucially, a more active engagement with the outdoors. But its modernist sensibilities are expressed in a voice that is textured and organic. Where rustic design traditionally has been about cave-like refuges (the log cabin with the overhanging eaves, the stone building with the small square windows, the hyper-vigilant focus on the hearth), rustic modern design displays an eagerness to engage with the world. Even in cases where the built environment takes the form of a retreat, its occupants are not retreating from the world but celebrating it. They may seek refuge from their worldly cares—rustic design inherently pursues this goal—but they are never closed off. There are no shut-ins in the rustic modern aesthetic.

The architecture of the rustic modern movement collaborates with the landscape; they are partners. It boldly employs materials that combine the organic with the cutting edge; it celebrates interiors that are clean, unfussy, and uncluttered; and it revels in

"ARCHITECTURE DOES CONTRIBUTE SO MUCH TO SENSE OF PLACE. IT CAN'T JUST BE NOSTALGIC, THOUGH. IT HAS TO HAVE SOME HONESTY IN THE TWENTY-FIRST CENTURY. BUT IT CAN STILL HAVE THAT TRUTH WITHIN A ROMANTIC CONTEXT."

—PAUL BERTELLI, JLF DESIGN BUILD

transitions between indoors and out that seamlessly blend the two. Windows are key in the new rustic modern. Those who love the landscape—whose spirits soar at the sight of the mountains, or are soothed by the still waters of a lake in the early morning light, or who thrill to the sight of breeching whales and breaking surf—want to maintain that connection always. The rustic modern home is not the place where one shuts the door and turns one's back to the elements. It is a vantage point—albeit a comfortable one—from which to engage in the elements.

This new approach to living in spectacular natural settings is finding a voice throughout the country's most beautiful and hallowed landscapes. Perhaps the greatest concentration of its practitioners may be in the Greater Yellowstone region, where talented designers, quality craftsmen, and clients with a sophisticated eye and love for the land come together in the shadow of some of the most stunning landscapes in the world. The best practitioners of this new aesthetic—from architects and designers to carpenters, stonemasons, blacksmiths, and furniture makers—are artists. The landowners who commit with intention to the process recognize this and bring their own passion to the projects. The result is architecture that is both soulful and exciting. It is grounded yet fresh, creative, and original—respectful of the land and regional styles yet poised on the edge of an ever-changing landscape of technological innovation. It honors and celebrates traditional crafts and techniques while embracing new efficiencies and methods. It is this fearless blending of both that defines rustic modern.

The homes can be highly engineered, employing state-of-the-art technologies in efficiency. They can be spare of line and free from unnecessary adornment. What they are not is modern for the sake of modern; there is no glass cube on an un-treed ski hill in these pages. There is instead a rebuilt mid-century A-frame house with glass end walls nestled on a promontory 600 feet above the crashing surf in one of the most iconic spots in the world; there is a twenty-first century farmhouse that references Montana's agricultural heritage but is reimagined for today; there is a mod *and* modest home which delights in surprises like bold color combinations and a climbing wall for access to its roof; and there is a diminutive home and guesthouse on an enormous conservation parcel—the structures were built to respect the sanctity of a landscape that sings with wildlife, old-growth live oaks, granite boulder gardens, natural springs, and ancient petroglyphs.

A contemporary adobe works within the design strictures of Santa Fe but asserts a strikingly current outlook, designed as it is around a significant collection of abstract Southwestern art. Three homes in Jackson Hole—all combining steel, glass, and reclaimed wood and making the most of the Teton views, while expressing very different interpretations—fully deliver on the promise of the new aesthetic.

A lakeside camp built by a leading architect and designed by him as his own personal retreat perfectly articulates the new vision of rustic modern; it reads rustic on first glance, but conveys a modernist sensibility in its details and in its outlook. There, as in all the highest expressions of the new rustic modern aesthetic, the structures are born of and tied to the land. They celebrate rather than domineer the site. They engage in constant dialogue with nature. There is no dynamic tension in the new rustic modern. Instead, there is an interplay.

INTENTIONAL MINIMALISM

In a modern house with a minimalist aesthetic, it's crucial that every choice, from materials to furnishings, be made with care and intention. This intentionality, when it governs the process from start to finish—from the crucial and lengthy pre-construction phase all the way through to the placement of the last art pieces—will be immediately apparent in the finished work. Then there is nothing loud, no one thing specifically demanding attention, even though the house may boast dramatic views, original expressions, and showstopping art. There is, rather, a suitability to site, an orchestrated sense of arrival, a beauty of line, a flow of movement, and a marrying together of all elements. When it works, the result is transcendent.

A residence in Jackson Hole, designed for a family of five plus their extended families and guests, represents the best of this intentional process. The collaborative partners were JLF Design Build and designer Arnelle Kase (who came out of retirement to help the clients, with whom she had worked previously) along with the thoughtful Bay Area couple who committed fully to the process, even through a yearlong move to France. The resulting house and guesthouse perfectly express the personality and meet the needs of its owners while maximizing the features of the site.

Jackson's valley floor is amply blessed with views, wildlife, and groundwater. The property (actually two lots joined together with their lot lines adjusted) boasts all these features, and the design team made the most of them. Logan Leachman, Paul Bertelli, and John Lauman of JLF designed a generously scaled and airy

▶ A Jackson Hole home by JLF Design Build was very intentional in its process. Designer Arnelle Kase and Heather Madden of Maya Design Studio furnished the rustic modern spaces with such finds as leather counter stools with blue-painted steel bases from Garza Marfa furniture studio in Marfa, Texas, and vintage milk glass pendant lights. It was the architect's idea to put the island on wheels.

▶▶ The open steel staircase with wood risers speaks to an industrial aesthetic while unique collectibles (the Indian tobacco bag atop the dining room buffet was purchased from Fighting Bear Antiques, the vintage cowboy portrait from Cayuse Western Americana) and custom designed laser-cut spiral wood pendants manifest the character of age and hand-crafted art.

yet intimate house and guesthouse overlooking a spring-fed pond. The main structure's somewhat meandering floor plan minimizes visual intrusions even as floor-to-ceiling windows in the living room maximize views of the Teton Range, Snake River Range, and Sleeping Indian mountain. An entry courtyard with a formal approach creates a sense of arrival for guests, but it is the family entry, accessed through a rustic handcrafted door at the base of a silo-like structure, that offers the first stunning surprise,

providing the exclamation point to the work. A spiral glass-and-steel staircase, viewed from underneath, has the opalescent beauty and hypnotic spiral of a seashell. It is also a sculptural presence that lifts one up, both literally and metaphorically. The staircase makes a dramatic statement, and offers a hint of both the originality of expression and consistently refined craftsmanship to be found throughout the house.

With the road on one side, some nearby neighbors, and the very steep ski mountain immediately

◄◄ The opalescent spiral staircase built by Scott Espelin of Wild West Ironworks has a transcendent beauty and serves a functional purpose—as well as acting as a primary conversation starter. Says JLF architect Logan Leachman, "It's a bit of an art piece, in and of itself."

◄ The silo structure serves as portal and hub, as well as the home's visual exclamation point. Upstairs, an antique spirit shield from the New Guinea Highlands exudes protective energy and marks the passage to bedrooms. The giant metal cage light fixture was custom designed through Coup D'Etat.

to the west, the architects worked to give each programmatic space some sense of separateness while orienting each toward a special view or outlook. The five-bedroom house spreads out, its varied roof heights and materials (some metal, some shake) minimizing its mass while lending a personality and sense of purpose. The silo acts as a hub through which all movement flows. The space is dramatic but functional; it houses a stylish mudroom, complete with individual lockers, and provides access to upstairs bedrooms. On one end of the structure, a two-story stone and weathered wood–clad guest wing faces views of the skier's mountain. The other, the master wing, almost like a separate cabin joined to the main house by a library/office, has its own porch with views to the south and Sleeping Indian mountain. The living room with dining area is an airy, steel-beamed and wood-floored expanse in which an open steel staircase with wood treads lends a modern industrial vibe. The adjoining kitchen has soaring high ceilings, unadorned steel trusses, and a wall of windows looking out to the mountains. A center island with a paperstone countertop is set on wheels, which lends a sense of whimsy while lightening its mass.

Visual surprises abound throughout the project, thanks to the collaborative collecting Arnelle Kase and her colleague Heather Madden engaged in with the clients over a period of several years. These include a tribal spirit shield from Papua New Guinea in the silo, a rifle-shaped neon sign hanging above the mudroom's metal lockers, a pair of Brazilian midcentury chairs in the living room, a hallway of framed tramp art collected on eBay and at antique shows, a hanging bed and beaded chair in the guesthouse, and an array of unusual lighting fixtures. An indoor/outdoor dining room with a stone floor and the feel of a screened porch has orange metal park chairs from the north of France and a hanging ship's ladder repurposed for wood storage. The master bedroom suite features three hand-stacked stone walls with small square windows and a stone ledge for art, in this case an original Edward S. Curtis photograph in a vintage frame displayed next to a small Southwestern pot. Immense book-matched live-edge redwood slabs mounted behind the headboard turn nature into art, as does a singular bathtub carved from a solid piece of Indonesian granite.

▲ Naturalistic landscaping and metal and wood exteriors help the home tread lightly on its Jackson Hole parcel.

▶ An indoor/outdoor dining room skillfully repurposes a vintage ship's ladder and Georgian courthouse lantern pendant light. Metal chairs originally from a provincial park in France add a generous dose of color and whimsy. James De Wulf designed the large, round concrete-and-steel dining table.

Despite all these wonders, the house has a minimalist feel. Kase and her clients chose each piece carefully and employed restraint throughout, resulting in a unique subtlety and elegance. "The style is much more personal," says Kase, who even made collages out of arrowheads for the house. "It reflects a world culture. The question was always, how can we bring a human hand to a new living space?"

The main home and guesthouse are carefully crafted inside and out and benefit from sophisticated technologies like geothermal wells, which use groundwater to heat and cool the structures. But the project architects credit the success of the house to the collaborative design-build process, which allowed the clients to leave the country for a full year while the process unfolded smoothly and still finished on time. "Our goal is to not surprise clients," explains JLF Design Build partner Logan Leachman. "We give them the tools to make informed decisions ahead of time."

It is the team approach, in which the architects serve as principal but where everyone has a voice, that allows for inspirations like the silo, which has become the hub of the home. "It's an art piece in and of itself," says Leachman. "It's the thing everyone is excited to talk about." And at the end of a day of skiing, fishing, or communing with nature, as an artistic statement that draws people in, pulls them together, and sparks conversation, it represents the best of modern rustic living.

◄◄ A tranquil guesthouse has its own aesthetic. In the sitting room the designers combined a bone-and-metal coffee table and carved ram's head with a couch and ottoman of their own design. The showstopping hand-beaded chair from Africa was purchased by the client and adds a striking graphic element to the space.

◄ The dining area features a porcelain antler light fixture, designed by Jason Miller for Roll & Hill, and a custom metal table with a repurposed industrial base. The opalescent glass globe pendant in the sitting area was purchased from Todd Donobedian Antiques.

◄ A midcentury desk from the client's private collection creates a focal point at the end of the guesthouse corridor. The vintage "Ant" chair is covered in hair-on hide.

▶ In the guest house bedroom with its subdued palette, a unique hanging bed designed by Arnelle Kase and Heather Madden and crafted by JW Sellars Furniture and Jeff Daly Metalwork offers a welcome visual surprise, as does a pair of charismatically shaggy stools.

MOUNTAIN MEETS MODERN

Ski houses are iconic in their way, but designing one poses two central dilemmas. The first is that the closer they are to the lifts, the better. Yet the closer they are to the lifts the harder it is to create a quiet refuge where the sights and sounds of a bustling ski resort fall away and nature still has a major impact. The second has to do with size. A ski house generally needs to be able to house extended families and host large gatherings, yet it also needs to feel cozy, even when only inhabited by one or two people. Finally, no matter how finished or refined the space, a ski house still needs to convey a put-your-booted-feet-up vibe.

Designer Tracey Byrne of the Waldyn Group had the opportunity to put all her theories into practice when designing a home for herself, her husband, Sam, and their children near Big Sky, Montana. First, they collaborated closely with architect Jerry Locati of Locati Architects to refine the floor plan and adapt some exterior materials (the house was already under construction). She then made it their own through her signature style, a European-influenced alpine modern look that celebrates a new kind of western. Her take is fresh, bold, and contemporary, yet still closely tied to the locale and the spectacular scenery visible though every window.

Residents of Massachusetts, the Byrnes had long been attracted to the mountain lifestyle. While raising their kids, they would make the long, often treacherous drive north on most weekends to ski at Sugarloaf Mountain in Maine. About ten years ago they visited the Big Sky area for the first time; once there, they fell hard for its dramatic wilderness landscape, understated glamour, and healthy outdoors-oriented lifestyle. They started spending time there, mostly as a winter destination, but over time as a summer destination, too, where they could hike for miles in the wilderness and play golf amidst mountain wildlife. As the couple

A burst of color in the entry via an abstract painting by Swiss artist Marta Oppikofer gives way to a more monochromatic palette in the living and dining areas. There texture reigns in custom chandeliers by Wish Design, a rustic wood table from Restoration Hardware, stacked stone, and weathered wood.

▲ Tracey Byrne envisioned the inviting seating area of her family's Locati Architects—designed ski house with an extra deep sectional and cozy sheepskin pillows. The graphic sheep painting by Adam Sakovy pops against a background of Montana barn board.

increasingly found work-related reasons to be there, they soon bought their first condo. Byrne decorated the home and was asked to help friends with theirs; it wasn't long before she was inundated with clients in the area, first redoing existing homes, then designing new construction.

Her own home is an expression of her ideas about livability in today's West. While a ski home does not have the same demands as a working ranch headquarters, nor an in-town year-round abode, it does have needs that should be met. In addition to such practicalities as how to make a home on a busy ski slope feel private yet still bring the outdoors in, or how to make a large house feel cozy, there are weather realities, lifestyle considerations (everyone in that climate needs a large and well-organized boot and gear room), and the fact that a ski house needs

to be able to expand and contract with the ebb and flow of guests but to do so seemingly effortlessly.

Byrne—who started out in banking then attended culinary school and became an artisan bread maker and bakery owner—is mostly self-taught in interior design. "I worked for an antique dealer part-time when my kids were young and it gave me some practical education," she says. "It doesn't come into play as much in Montana, but it was a great foundation for [understanding] shape and scale. Scale is really important; it always bothers me seeing something that's too small for a space."

The designer favors cooler whites over warmer whites and although she loves color, she believes it's best to keep a room's palette more muted, injecting the life that strong color brings through accessories and art. She gets a lot of her ideas from travel, such as when antiquing in Europe. She likes finding a treasure, like a traditional chair frame at a Paris flea market, then covering it with something unexpected such as cowhide, giving it a contemporary flair. Byrne says she has made mistakes but has learned from them. And, she says, "I'm good at knowing what I don't like; I've been told by builders that I'm easy to work with."

Architect Jerry Locati would agree. He and Byrne collaborated on the final design of the three-level slope-side home, adjusting some interior walls and maximizing the views for the public spaces. (Byrne believes bedrooms should have some intimacy, and that they don't need to claim the best views in the house.) Locati says the home's views are its most impressive feature. To balance that, he designed for a sense of arrival, with heated stairs and interesting lighting leading from the garage level to a welcoming terrace to the front door.

Stone treatment was used as a unifying connective element, while once inside, a central stairwell connects the different levels of the home. Large windows and an outdoor living/dining area with a fireplace off the kitchen bring in light, open the house to the views, and amplify the indoor/outdoor experience.

In excess of 7,000 square feet and with six bedrooms to accommodate large numbers, the house is extensive. But Byrne made the spaces welcoming, humanly scaled, and livable through a deft mix of traditional stone and wood and more modern metallic or midcentury type designs; a muted palette with strategically placed bursts of color and textural pieces adding vibrancy and depth to the furnishings; large, somewhat bold contemporary art pieces; oversized couches; and statement lighting fixtures.

Locati points out that Byrne's use of stone, steel, and timber is not new, but "the interpretation is more clean and contemporary." In the master bedroom, for instance, multicolored reclaimed snow fencing covers the wall behind the bed frame, climbs the ceiling to the ridgeline, and comes down the other side to cover the wall next to the stone hearth. This effect is offset by the end wall, which remains white. The room—with its traditional western rustic materials like wood, stone, and sheepskin, its unexpected shiny metallic bed frame, a heavily tufted sheepskin rug, and a large, twiggy chandelier—balances all the elements perfectly: modern and classic, shiny hard and tufted soft, rustic and contemporary. The white

▲ An outdoor room, with its fireplace, camp chairs, and generously sized table, can be used year round.

▶ A seating group has its attention focused outside. Sheepskin covered stools on narrow legs can be easily moved; leather armchairs offer comfortable seating for reading and relaxing.

◄ The built-in leather banquette seating, made to Byrne's specifications by Green Seams Design in Bozeman, was deliberately elevated so that diners could watch the skiers passing by.

► The expansive kitchen was designed for large family gatherings and for frequent entertaining. Designer Tracey Byrne says, "I love black. It grounds the cabinets in this very big room." The lighting fixtures suspended over the double islands are from Vaughan.

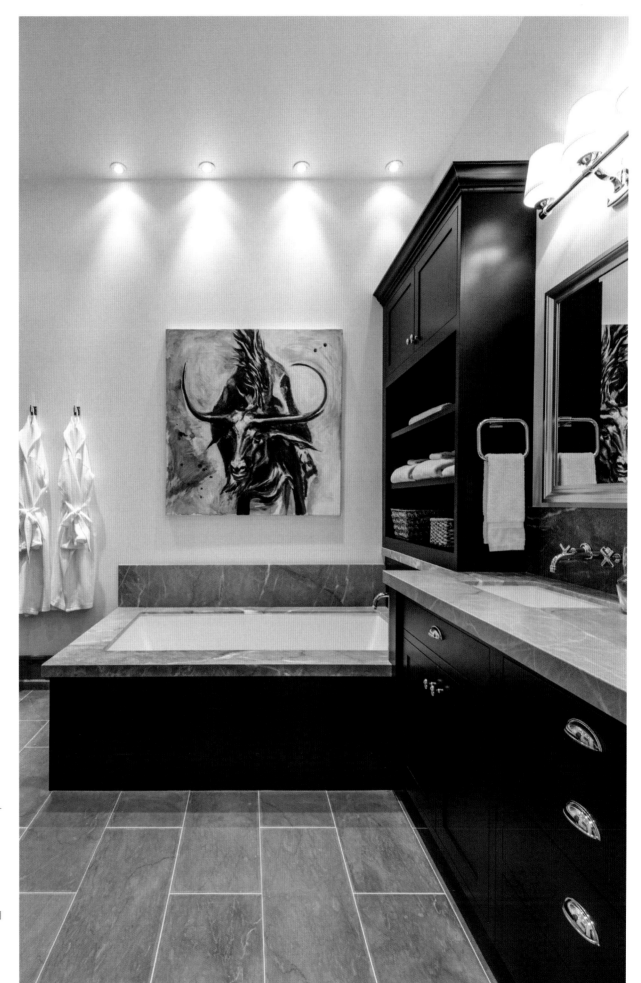

◄ An arrangement of ceramic antlers against a wall of weathered barn boards and a grouping of metallic objects on a traditional sideboard skill-fully bridge the rustic modern divide.

▶ Dark cabinetry, gray tones, and white walls create a clean palette while a vintage painting of a bull—a traditional western subject rendered in a contemporary hand—injects energy into an otherwise serene master bath.

wall balances the weathered wood while an ethereal lighting fixture floats above it all.

The balancing act is achieved in every room, from the oversized kitchen, with its double islands and black cabinetry, to the bedrooms and bunk room. In each room, explains Locati, "It all plays together rather than your eye being drawn to one spot. It works well and comes off with very clean lines. But," he adds, "you don't ever forget you're in Montana."

▲ The bunk room with built-in beds finished in weathered wood combines rustic finishes with a refined chest of drawers and a contemporary-leaning black ladder.

▶ The wood treatment in the master bedroom delivers an unexpected surprise when it travels up and over the ceiling. A quiet combination of cream and gray tones creates a restful refuge, while the chrome bed delivers a touch of glam. The twig chandelier is by Wish Design; the hand-made Flokati rug is from the Sheepskin Factory.

CALIFORNIA CONSERVATION NARRATIVE

California's Gaviota Coast is known for its extreme natural beauty and untouched ruggedness. It is a region of steep scrub-covered hills, impossibly curvy roads, limitless views, and soaring condors. While its cultural center, Santa Barbara, is the very definition of well groomed (note lush estates, polo fields, golf courses, and vineyards), one doesn't have to venture far beyond its landscaped edges to discover surrounding areas that are remarkably wild.

Montana resident Deborah Van Dyke wasn't looking for a part-time home when she first visited the area almost twenty years ago for a nonprofit board meeting. But she immediately felt drawn to its special qualities of light and weather and landscape. This feeling only intensified on her subsequent trips, ultimately translating to action when she visited the property known as Rancho Dos Vistas.

As the name implies, the most striking thing about the site is its views. The 1,440-acre parcel commands almost two miles of ridgeline, affording unending vistas over the ocean. In the foreground lie the Channel Islands; in the distance one sees the curve of the earth. At times the sun sparkles on the water where, with the aid of binoculars, one can see surfers, whales, and sailboats. At other times a layer of fog hugs the lowlands, creating an otherworldly feeling of seclusion. What's most unusual about the site is that it also offers views into the Santa Ynez Valley. On one side lies the vast expanse of the Pacific Ocean, sparkling under the sun or blanketed by fog; on the other a pastoral

▶ The owner's goal for a rebuilt bungalow on a large conservation property on California's Gaviota Coast was to keep the interiors airy, light, clean, and simple. The living room can be opened up to the outdoors with double doors on either side of the building, but on wintry days the central hearth is the focus. The vintage leather club chairs are French; the built-in bench does double duty as a firewood storage chest.

▶▶ The owner chose simple clean-lined furniture for the partially covered patio to keep the focus on the garden-like grove of live oaks.

landscape of orchards and ranchlands surrounded by precipitous, picturesque mountains.

Rancho Dos Vistas seems a world away, perched as it is on top of the ridge, where in the daytime it hovers above the bustle and at night is held up under the brilliance of the night sky. The property is adjacent to former President Reagan's Rancho del Cielo, yet is even larger and more remote. Forty miles of roads and trails access every part of the property, whose hillsides are covered with manzanita, with their bell-like flowers, and strewn with boulders, in some places resembling a rock garden. The ranch features natural springs and a year-round creek, nurturing an unusually lush landscape for such an arid region, as well as a lake stocked with fish. Thousands of live oaks, with their sculptural shapes, and madrone, with their red bark, create an ethereal habitat that is perfect for varied birdlife such as songbirds, ducks, and quail, as well as deer, bobcat, and even the occasional cougar. In the spring

there is an abundance of wildflowers: buttercups, monkey flowers, shooting stars, Indian paintbrush. The property also has numerous caves. While there have been only four recorded deed-holders, clearly the site has held significance for generations. Local lore says the land was traversed by the Chumash Indians; one of the caves guards petroglyphs.

It is no surprise, then, that Van Dyke became enamored of the site on her very first visit, and that upon purchasing the ranch, her first instinct was to preserve it. A preexisting conservation easement through the Land Trust for Santa Barbara County meant that the land was already well protected; strict county regulations for new construction in addition to the easement mandated that Van Dyke would adhere to the existing footprints of the property's modest structures. This suited her purposes perfectly.

An existing two-bedroom structure, of utilitarian construction and probably built in the 1960s,

◄ The L-shaped main structure, nestled amidst ancient
oak trees and massive granite
boulders, adheres to its original footprint and makes the
most of available shade in the
hot, dry climate. The owner
kept the original stucco look
on the exterior but added a
metal roof to limit fire danger.

▲ The patio dramatizes the
home's ridgetop siting with
limitless views of the Channel
Islands and Pacific Ocean—or
across the top of a fogbank.

offered a usable shell. There was also a storage shed
that might have been used as a bunkhouse back in
the days when the property was a cattle ranch. Not
only was it uninhabitable, it was lacking a floor. Both
needed to be gutted and remade, but Van Dyke saw
their potential.

"The main house was really just an adobe shell
with a big fireplace; it wasn't really livable," says Van
Dyke. It is now a one-bedroom adobe home centered
on the large fireplace. Van Dyke worked with Santa
Barbara architect Thomas Ochsner on all designs.
They installed a new kitchen, laundry room, patio,
and floors and punched additional windows and
doors to open the home to the extraordinary views.
They replaced an unsound roof with one of bonderized standing-seam metal, a choice both aesthetically
pleasing and, in an area of high fire danger, emi-
nently sensible. The owner, who lives most of the
year in a traditional log building, fell in love with the
simplicity of the home and the contrast between the
styles. After all the exposed wood in her Montana
home, she says, "I was really into the clean lines of
an adobe. And it was fun to do something that was
both old and modern."

Van Dyke furnished both structures with pieces
purchased from local antique shops or crafted to
her specifications. She identified local artists whose

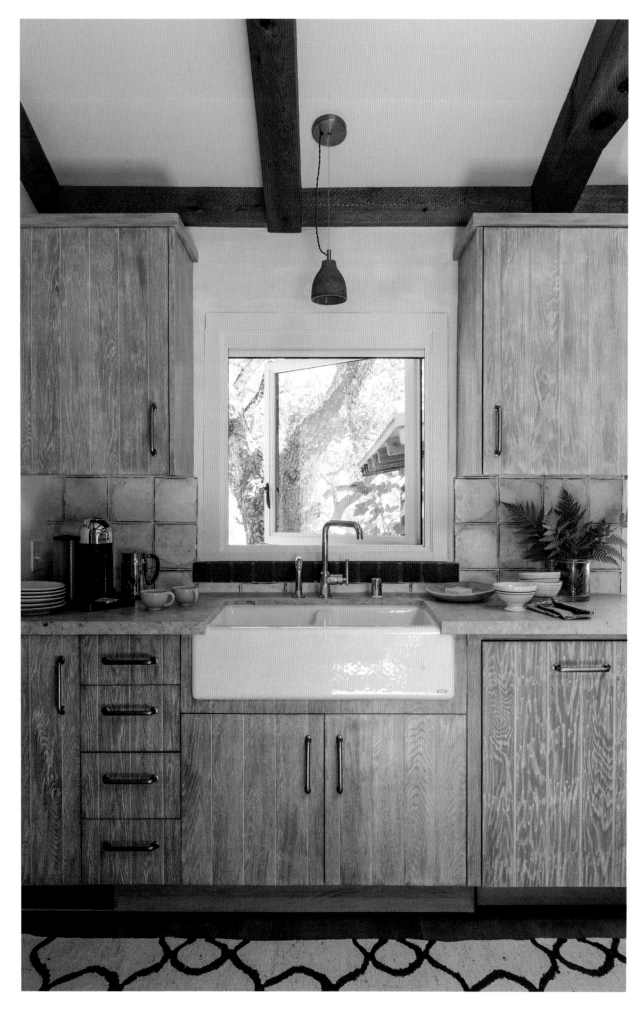

◀ The updated country kitchen is light and airy with cabinets inspired by a modernist kitchen seen in a Danish architecture book and crafted locally. The brick windowsill above the harvest sink was original to the house.

▶ A kitchen island has a butcher block top on a stainless steel base on wheels; it rests under a preexisting skylight which floods the room with natural light. The tiles, sourced locally, are French. The hanging lamp is concrete.

work she liked and had a chandelier made that was inspired by a piece she saw in a magazine. She knew she wanted a kitchen with clean lines and an airy quality. She chose cabinets with a modern, fresh feel and a stainless steel oven and hood, installed marble countertops with embedded sea creatures, and, in place of an island, selected a butcher block table on a rolling stainless steel base. She chose a limestone-topped round dining table to contrast with the wood in the house, found hand-painted kitchen tiles at a local tile store, and sourced interesting but reasonably priced concrete lighting fixtures from England. The oversized beams and framing around the windows and doors are of northern red cedar from the Pacific Northwest, which builder Thomas Allin liked for its subtle red, green, and purple hues.

Although the home's sense of arrival is restrained—in keeping with the simplicity of the house and the grandeur of the setting—Van Dyke did expand the original narrow entry to a set of double doors for a more welcoming aspect. On the opposite side, overlooking the top-of-the-world view, a partially covered flagstone patio extends the living space substantially while allowing the focus to remain on the vistas.

The nearby casita, which was completed simultaneously, is a long narrow building with one bedroom, a sitting room that can serve as a second bedroom, and an ample patio. It has whitewashed walls, wood ceilings and floors, and large windows that fill the room with soft light filtered through the surrounding oaks. "It was the perfect size for a guesthouse," says Van Dyke. "I wanted to keep it small, simple, elegant."

With both homes, Van Dyke achieved her goals, to create a quiet, comfortable yet restrained refuge where the focus remains on the extraordinary landscape and where one's gaze is constantly directed outside. She achieved what she set out to do: to build in harmony with the setting and with respect for the unique aspects of this special property high above the sea. She is, after all, merely its steward.

The open dining area—with stone table, custom-made dining chairs, and a live-edge bar—is dominated by a painting of the moon setting over the ocean by local artist and native South African Karen Bezuidenhout.

The long, narrow, one-bedroom guest casita has a living room with pull-out couch and opens to the outdoors on two sides. A painting by Karen Bezuidenhout hangs over a handcrafted breakfast bar. The chair is one of a pair the owner found at a Montecito antique shop and had restored.

SPORTY
MOD HOME

East Jackson may be the last holdout in a town besieged by the highest real estate prices in the country. An older neighborhood of modest ranch homes with very few remaining buildable lots, it is an area in transition, slowly succumbing to the inevitable gentrification of one of the West's most glamorous destinations.

With change comes evolution, a point proven by a new addition to the neighborhood. In design (boxy), materials (metal), window placement (nontraditional), and spirit (bold interior colors and a twenty-seven-foot climbing wall), the home represents a decidedly modern take on new western living.

In a way, the homeowner had been doing her research for years. As a longtime western lifestyle, design, and travel writer/editor, Dina Mishev had had ample time to ponder the art of living, develop her palate, and refine her aesthetic. She moved to Jackson from the East Coast by way of college in the Midwest. She originally gravitated to the country's steepest mountain in order to become a double black diamond skier. She refers to herself as "the world's worst ski bum," because not only did she already have a 9-to-5 paralegal job lined up, she was unaware of the proximity of Grand Teton National Park. As quickly as she had moved to Wyoming, though, she ditched her well-laid plans. Within a couple of weeks, her intention to attend law school went out the window. And it soon became evident that her year in Jackson, characterized by a rekindled passion for the outdoors (she skis a stunning one hundred days a year), had turned into a life move.

Over a fifteen-year period, Mishev lived in a succession of dwellings, each a slight improvement over the last. In 2007 she and her then husband bought an empty lot in east Jackson. The real estate market was daunting, and east Jackson, though more densely settled than some areas in the valley, was no exception.

But it had huge appeal for a dual-career couple living in the valley year round. It is within walking distance to town; it's also close to Snow King, the locals' mountain, and the Cache Creek trailhead. The couple's original intention was to build on the entire lot, but life got in the way, during which time the market changed radically. Once things had settled down again, Mishev was the sole owner of a subdivided lot. Then, in 2013, she recalls, "I felt like I was in a rut." Within six weeks, she had met with Eric Logan of Carney Logan Burke Architects to discuss designing a house. Immediately afterwards, she recalls, "I rented out my condo for two months and decided to go ski and climb a really big mountain in Asia."

In a testament to her faith in her vision and the reliability of her team, she agreed on the home's design with architect Eric Logan, hired contractor Kevin Patno of Patno Construction, rented out her condo, and embarked on her adventure. The goal was to break ground as soon as she returned.

Logan describes the project as "us trying to wring as much as possible from the budget and the site. The approach from an architecture and planning standpoint was to keep it very simple. That meant: don't make the structure complicated. The project could gain complexity, but we wanted to start simply with a two-story box."

An initial—and crucial—decision from which all else followed was to create an upside-down design, placing the home's public rooms on the second floor. This allowed for selective vistas through creative window placement, which was essential in order to maximize privacy while opening up the home to views of Snow King, the Tetons, and the Gros Ventre mountains, the range that acts as Jackson Hole's eastern boundary. It also allowed for openings in the so-called box to create exterior living spaces that accessed the views and the outdoors without being hemmed in and overshadowed by the neighbors.

The house was small by design. "I didn't want much space," says the owner. "I appreciate efficiency, and small mandates that." She did have some specifications—she wanted an office, a guest room and, for the first time in her life, her own garage—but was open to suggestions for everything else, such as the exterior.

Mishev was happy with the initial drawing Logan showed her, requesting only one small modification:

High ceilings and polished concrete floors create a feeling of volume which is exaggerated by the room's lack of unnecessary architectural detail, thin profile quartz stone countertops, open back Kartell Masters counter stools, a transparent coffee table, and Victoria "Ghost" chairs. A burst of color in the backsplash of glass subway tiles enlivens the otherwise sedate room, while the wave-like under-counter treatment from ModWalls adds organic interest.

to create a powder room upstairs located as far away from the dining table as possible. With the public rooms on the second floor, there was the question of how to handle access. After consultation, Logan chose to set the stairwell on the south side of the house for its quality of light, then designed "cat-scratch windows" that cast an interesting pattern of shadows all day long.

Mishev discussed the budget with her contractor then set off on her trip. Many weeks later and once off the mountain, Mishev made her way to Kashgar, China, where she had a Skype session with both architect and contractor. One week after her return to Jackson, they broke ground.

With construction under way, Mishev was excited to select her color palette and design her interiors. After writing about design for years, she had some ideas. She chose green glass tiles for the kitchen back-splash as her starting point, and used the same color downstairs on the walls of her office. Her use of bold blue and orange on some walls (with trim painted the same color as the rooms, to make it disappear), offset

Homeowner Dina Mishev's bold color choices throughout the house brighten and energize the spaces during Jackson Hole's occasional blizzards. In such a minimalist interior, the colorful zigzag fabric shade of YLighting's Missy suspension light stands out as a graceful artistic statement. The large format artwork is by Monica Aiello, a painter inspired by geological processes.

◄ A more subdued shade of blue is appropriate for a room devoted to repose. The white resin moose head represents a playful nod to regional mores.

▶ The homeowner made thoughtful budgetary decisions on items like Ikea cabinets, then devoted significant resources to important focal points such as lighting. The dramatic Ango Cascade Suspension Light from YLighting—inspired by and comprised of silkworm cocoons—lights the way for visitors to this upstairs/down-stairs house and does double duty as a hanging sculpture.

by white ceilings, lends vibrancy to the space, especially in the winter when light levels are low.

"Color is the most exciting thing for me," she says. "I thought I was using quite a bit of restraint because in my condo there wasn't a single neutral color. In this house I have a neutral color on some of the walls; when I wanted a neutral, I used the same one throughout the home. I was proud of myself for not putting color on every single wall, but then the painters said they'd never seen so many colors in one house before."

Mishev was able to wring the most out of her budget by choosing all the fixtures herself and weighing her choices carefully. But she happily blew her budget on light fixtures. These, she points out, can transform a space.

The outdoor rooms, one private, one public, enhance the home immeasurably. The deck off the master bedroom enjoys the morning light from the east and looks out over one of the owner's favorite hikes. The second deck doubles the square footage of the living room. Partly protected from the sun and weather by an overhang, it gets a lot of use for dinner parties and is a great place for a nap in a hammock. For her dog and cat, it offers the perfect sunbathing spot while providing a strategic vantage point over the neighborhood.

One of the home's most arresting features, the outdoor climbing wall, was a spontaneous decision as well as a practical solution to the question of how to access the roof. While the remainder of the house is clad in black corrugated metal, the climbing wall is made of five-foot-wide strips of plywood painted black; colorful purchased climbing holds are affixed to the plywood. It being Jackson Hole, of course contractor Kevin Patno is also a climber; he placed the holds so the climb would be challenging but manageable, and allowed for more than one route to the top.

Mishev's years of writing about other people's design projects proved invaluable as she assembled her team, crafted her budget, and chose her color palette, fixtures, and furnishings with decisiveness and authority. Small does not mean easy, yet the entire process was completed in nine months, a blink of the eye by home-construction standards.

"I've been writing about Carney Logan Burke projects for over a decade," she reflects. "It helped that they knew me and knew my personality."

It also helped that she instinctively knew how to design small to live large.

◀◀ Mishev's skillful juxtaposition of color and minimal detailing create vibrant transitions between living spaces.

▲ Strategically placed windows allow carefully edited views of the nearby mountains while screening neighbors' homes. White pendant lights pop against colorful walls and add a sculptural, organic touch to the interiors. Light fixtures, says the homeowner, can transform a space.

COASTAL AERIE

When Nathaniel Owings proposed to Margaret Wentworth, he was an internationally prominent architect and a founder of one of the largest architecture firms in the world. He had chosen his moment: they were picnicking on peaches and champagne atop a precipitous rocky ridge 600 feet above the surf in Big Sur. Her conditions for accepting his proposal—that he build her a house on that very spot—became the basis of a unique love story, and the catalyst for one of the most iconic homes on the California coast.

Dubbed Wild Bird for its gravity-defying siting, upon its completion in 1958 the house was named "the most beautiful house on the most beautiful site" in the US by *TIME* magazine. Designed by architect Mark Mills under Nathaniel Owings' direction, it was conceived as a simple A-frame, with floor-to-ceiling glass on either end to allow unimpeded views up and down the coastline. The house was small and snug, built not for large gatherings or a showy presence, but for two people with a conservation ethos. It was an immediate success, both as a coastal and architectural landmark and as a home from which the couple became as deeply attached to the region as the house was rooted to the land. Although intended as the Owings' vacation home, it, and Big Sur, drew them in; they spent increasing amounts of time there and Margaret settled there permanently after Nathaniel's death in 1984. Both Owingses were intimately involved in the movement to preserve the special character and wild nature of the area. Nathaniel and Margaret, with input from Skidmore Owings & Merrill, drafted the 1960 Big Sur Land Use Plan, the original coastal protection master plan. Margaret was an ardent environmentalist on many fronts. Upon her death in 1999, the *New York*

◄ An iconic midcentury cliff-top house in Big Sur, originally designed by architect Mark Miller for internationally renowned architect Nathaniel Owings and his bride, has been restored and updated for the twenty-first century.

► Dan Fletcher of Fletcher & Hardoin Architects was able to preserve the home's original concrete beams, as well as its distinctive A-frame profile, visible from Highway 1.

Times described her as "a California artist and conservationist who fought for the survival of sea otters, sea lions, mountain lions, and other wild creatures."

It seems fitting, then, that Wild Bird, despite having now been rebuilt for the twenty-first century, has never lost sight of its original design or intention, much as Big Sur itself (a handful of restaurants, inns, galleries, state parks, and a public library tucked among the redwoods and strung along a sixty-five-mile stretch of Highway 1) is virtually unchanged. Today the primary A-frame structure appears from Highway 1 as it did in the Owings' day. And to visit Wild Bird still means having an almost overwhelming nature experience. Although the house is tucked within the few trees hardy enough to find purchase

▲ An unrestrained use of glass makes the most of the aerie-like main guest quarters. Architect Dan Fletcher said he wanted to re-create what it might feel like to be a condor perched on a redwood tree.

▶ Originally the site of Margaret Owings' art studio, the guesthouse makes the most of its placement. Shielded from the view of Highway 1 drivers by the few hardy trees that cling to the rocky cliff, the room is all about the views across the open ocean.

In its twenty-first-century iteration, the home celebrates the indoor/outdoor relationship, with every room opened up to nature and the views.

on the rocky promontory, from every room the vastness of the ocean and the ruggedness of the coastline are stunningly immediate. To stand on the small terrace with its transparent wall at the edge of the cliff is to be held aloft high above the waves, with an unimpeded view up and down the iconic Big Sur coastline and across the ocean to the curved horizon, listening to the constant barking from the seal rookery on the boulders below, with California condors circling above, sea birds diving below, and the intermittent surfacing of whales, porpoises, and sea otters. To witness this festival of nature as the sun slowly drops into the sea is an experience nothing short of sublime.

It was this promise that prompted an English businessman with a longtime interest in the area to purchase the property, practically sight unseen, in 2000. He bought it somewhat as a birthday surprise for his wife, who loved the area; herself a hotelier,

◀ A subdued modernist treatment around the hearth provides a focal point on foggy indoor days without detracting from the views on clear days.

▶ Sleek cabinetry and fixtures anchor the kitchen, where one wall of glass overlooks the view down the coastline. A glass door to another, more protected patio provides access to a built-in grill and outdoor dining area.

she counted nearby Ventana Inn as one of her favorite hotels in the world. But when they first viewed Wild Bird prior to the purchase, he recalls, "I fell in love with it. She hated it."

The house was in poor shape. "It was completely run down," says the owner. "There were voles, mice, rats. The kitchen was from the 1950s. The woodwork in the studio was all broken up. There was almost no plumbing and the basement was solid concrete with little slits for light. My wife said, 'It's magical, but I'd rather stay at Ventana.'"

"Everyone was aware the house needed to be renovated," says longtime local and informal advisor Ken Wright, who first met the couple at the time of the purchase. "It leaked like a sieve in storms, and was drafty and cold." Margaret Owings, who had died there at age eighty-five, had spent her last years

▲ Margaret Owings was an artist as well as a conservationist. Her "Wild Bird" mosaic occupies pride of place at Wild Bird today.

▶ A dramatic, cliff's-edge patio with an outdoor fireplace and infinity-edge spa offers the perfect vantage point for observing whales and watching the sun slowly sink into the ocean.

▲ Floor-to-ceiling glass in the master bedroom and a glass corner in the master bath dramatize Wild Bird's siting atop a knife-edged promontory 600 feet above the crashing surf.

directing her resources toward saving sea otters and mountain lions rather than home repairs. Skylights leaked, concrete was flaking, single-paned windows let the wind through, and water would seep up through the rocks on which the house was built. "More than once I was down there cobbling something together to make sure Margaret was dry and had firewood," Wright recalls.

Despite the home's state of disrepair, and the difficulty of working on a narrow granite cliff edge, the Englishman was undaunted. "This was not an acquisition to own something," Wright recalls. "This was an acquisition because he truly loved and believed in it. He was exuberant."

The owner set about assembling the Wild Bird team: Dan Fletcher of Fletcher & Hardoin Architects; Steven Hensel for interior design, with subsequent updates done by Linda Lamb of Lamb Design Group; David Stocker of Stocker & Allaire General Contractors; and landscape designer Ron Herman, who would select a palette of drought-tolerant native plants.

The owner's main goal was to increase the size of the house to accommodate a family of six while preserving the home's iconic appearance, respecting the landscape and acting "in sympathy with what Nat Owings and Mark Mills would have wanted," according to architect Dan Fletcher. He was keenly aware that the house, though not designated as historic, "was forty-seven years old and was nonetheless a house of great note and design. I did a lot of research and got a local historian involved early on. As a designer, I thought, 'If this were being done today, how would the original designers have brought it into this century?'"

Although the project was a remodel (the footprint and much of the layout remained the same), the conditions were daunting. Contractor David Stocker had the challenge of undertaking the work on a steep, narrow, precipitous site with a minimal staging area plagued by high winds and winter storms. To make matters more interesting, the timing of the project coincided with the successful reintroduction of California condors to the nearby

▲ A curving path from the guest apartment and garage emphasizes its relationship with nature by clinging to the contours of the hill.

Ventana Wilderness. The enormous adolescent birds—curious and highly destructive—treated the protective scaffolding as a giant cliff's edge jungle gym and wreaked havoc with landscaping, tools, materials, and more than one tractor seat.

Not much of the home was actually salvageable, beyond the original redwood beams of the roof and the concrete beams that support it, and some of Margaret Owings' wonderful period ceramics. Although the size of an adjacent bedroom suite on the south side of the garage is slightly larger than the original, the garage was downsized and given a green roof, thereby actually shrinking the home's profile from the road. An existing structure just below the A-frame (Margaret Owings' art studio, which Wright describes as "very funky and run down"), became a spectacular guesthouse: a glass-walled box that is tucked into the trees yet has the feel of an aerie overlooking a vast expanse of sea.

Construction completed, the house is as wild as ever. In addition to the nonstop carnival of marine mammals below, red-tail hawks, hummingbirds, rattlesnakes, and scorpions are abundant, and ring-tailed cats have been known to enter through the kitchen windows to dine from the larder. Winter storms are intense; they can dislodge rocks and generate mudslides that block Highway 1 and even cut off access to the driveway. Given the aridity and inaccessibility of the surrounding Los Padres National Forest, it is not unusual to be evacuated due to wildfires.

Though the project took many years to complete, the team's purpose, defined by the original vision of Nathaniel and Margaret Owings, remained true. "That house represents a great collaborative process," says architect Dan Fletcher. "Everyone worked really hard to make this house a very, very special place."

"I believe it's a very successful renovation of an iconic property that happens to be in one of the most beautiful places in the world," agrees Ken Wright. "When I look at this house, I see the same structure that was there before. And it's as beautiful today as it ever was.

"I think that Nathaniel and Margaret—especially Margaret, who was so in love with the site—would totally approve of what the owners have done with this property, based on so many conversations that took place at two in the morning," Wright adds. "It was not unusual to talk about the feeling of specialness that was there. That feeling is still there."

LAKESIDE RUSTIC

When an architect known for designing beautiful rustic homes in spectacular natural settings sits down to design a retreat for himself, it is bound to be a very intentional, intensely personal process. Larry Pearson of Pearson Design Group has an in-town home and a new Bozeman office for his architecture firm. When he thought about building a lakeside getaway for himself, his kids, and his friends, he wanted to have the best of both worlds: he was seeking a laid-back feel and full immersion in nature, yet because of his busy lifestyle he wanted to be close enough to town so that once there he would never have to pick up the car keys.

The site he selected, ten acres on the northeastern tip of thirty-two-mile-long Flathead Lake, is semi-wetland. Usually partly under water, it is lush with native grasses, birch, spruce, and cottonwoods and alive with birdlife such as osprey, hawks, and songbirds. It is not unusual to see fox kits hopping through the grass and fawns bedded down with their mothers. At night the great expanse of lake and low levels of light pollution create a perfect setting for star gazing, while the lakeside setting provides ample opportunity for sporty water activities. Better yet, the property is close enough to Big Fork to walk into town, but still perfectly positioned for spectacular views of the dramatic summer lightning storms that sweep up the length of the lake.

Pearson had owned a generously scaled lake home before. For this project, he wanted to create a true retreat. An aficionado of modern design, he was envisioning a small and rather minimal modernist main structure; more than anything, he wanted a camp-like feel. He drew—and discarded—many designs, he recalls. "I went back and forth between a modern and 'lake country' design, but

▶ A rustic camp built on a ten-acre site on Flathead Lake by architect Larry Pearson for his own family and friends is the ultimate rustic modern getaway.

▶▶ Simplicity reigns in the metal, glass, and weathered-wood exterior and in the choice of furnishings: a mix of found objects, custom-crafted items, and materials taken from the site.

I thought I'd never feel the casual vibe I wanted if it was too contemporary. I decided to split the difference, to find something that communicated both languages." The result, he says, "is that it has a clean but casual feel that we all want in a lake cabin."

The experience begins prior to the approach to the compound, at the car park a thousand feet from the house. The visitor leaves the car behind and carries his or her belongings along a curving wooden boardwalk through the grasses, past a striking obelisk-like trio of sculpted standing tree trunks to the encampment. The house, dock, fire pit, and picnic area with festive strung lights, a tepee, Airstream trailer, and boathouse (which also serves as a game room, overflow area, and work space with drafting table), adhere to an understated minimalist ethos. Each relates to the next in a harmonious but restrained way. The result is a true lake camp where indoor/outdoor living is perfectly balanced and the mood is always relaxed.

The cabin has two parts. The taller portion has two bedrooms overlooking the lake, stacked in a box form; an adjoining one-level mass with a vaulted ceiling houses the kitchen, dining room, and living room. A screened porch with reclaimed barn wood walls, a floating orb-like wood-burning stove, and large windows on three sides acts as a transitional space between indoors and out. Pearson says he chose the bonderized metal roof because it is indestructible, and juxtaposed steel headers and knee braces against gray-toned aged barn wood siding.

A short stroll away and perched on the edge of the lake is the more rustic one-room boathouse. It acts as a second living room as well as an office for the architect; it houses a drafting table so that he can design when he feels inspired. The building is heated and insulated, but, in keeping with the camp atmosphere, it is designed to look as though it's not. Wallboards turned on the diagonal add texture and a sense of fun while differentiating it from the main house. A generous covered area creates an outdoor dining room. Sheltered from sun and rain, it further blurs the transition between indoors and out.

Both main house and boathouse have whitewashed walls and ceilings and darker wood floors, with warmer-toned ceilings rendering the spaces less austere. In the main house, steel I-beams with visible writing and a bit of rust lend an industrial

◄ A long, low shed-like structure attaches to a two-story
bedroom tower. Set back from
the lake and partially shielded
by trees, the home blends
into its environment yet still
maintains spectacular views
along the length of the thirty-
two-mile lake.

▲ An airy open kitchen blends
the simple summer cabin look
of whitewashed wood with
an unadorned steel beam,
glass accents, and a cabinet,
chairs, and pendants from
Restoration Hardware. The
legs of the dining table were
made from wood found on the
property.

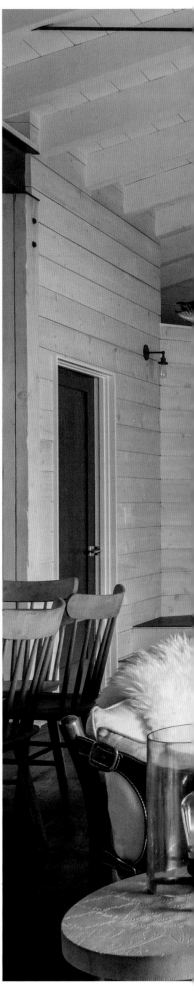

edge, while the stairway's driftwood newel posts, collected on the property, bring the outdoors in. Furnishings combine farmhouse-type pieces with vintage midcentury modern designs. In the kitchen, minimal open shelving maintains the light, airy feel of the public spaces.

The interiors department at Pearson, led by designer Leisa Kolstad, created a sense of retreat and simplicity. Kolstad worked toward a casual and informal feeling with a clean, minimal, and collected approach on the furnishings. Travis Denman from Denman Construction collaborated with Pearson from the beginning of the design process to help develop and deliver the retreat. His team of contractors was able to put Pearson's vision into reality. In the end, a home with modernist leanings and steel details still feels like a humble, simplistic cabin.

Pearson's intention is a carefully calibrated experience designed so that one's worldly cares recede with each step away from the car. This is achieved with one's arrival across the boardwalk, walking past the trio of tapered logs to the buildings and outdoor living spaces. As the visitor approaches the camp and is encompassed by the power of the lake, the landscape, and the sky, nature asserts itself and the world falls away—neatly fulfilling the promise of a lakeside camp, and the very definition of retreat.

▲ The ground-floor bedroom draws the color of the lake and sky into the room through the rug, artwork, and ottomans. A sheepskin throw injects warmth into a relatively sparse interior.

▶ Reminders of nature abound in the casual but studied interiors. Newel posts were fashioned from driftwood found on site. The teak root table lends organic interest. Touches of blue in rugs throughout both structures speak to the lake and sky.

In summertime, the doors between the living room and screened porch swing wide to enhance an open camp-like feel. The sofa and chair are both vintage, by Swedish designer Arne Norell. Ottomans from Roost add texture to the interior.

◀ The home's rustic modern ethos is perfectly captured in the suspended wood-burning stove. A striped rug, wicker rocking chair, and Pendleton blanket enhance the summer camp feel. A pair of found stools can be tucked under the metal-topped dining table made by Sandmeyer Design. The table legs were made from wood that was found on the property then charred using a Japanese technique called Shou Sugi Ban.

▲ Throughout the compound, the emphasis is on the site's relationship to the lake. String lights, a tepee, and natural seating expand the usable space.

▲ A one-room, single-story boathouse has an entire wall of windows to emphasize the structure's relationship to the water. Furnishings include a Verellen couch, Ralph Lauren chairs, collected items found at High Point Market in North Carolina, and a woven pendant, which ties the room to the natural world.

◀ A low-profile boardwalk-like dock physically links the boathouse to the lake.

▶ Pearson uses the room as a workspace—the natural light is great for drafting—and for guest overflow when necessary.

▲ The relationship between boathouse and water is evident in the exterior boardwalk that becomes the dock. A custom-crafted metal fire pit provides another spot to hang out in the open air. Seating is simple and natural.

▶ As an architect, Larry Pearson thinks through every aspect of the experience, starting with an orchestrated arrival. At his lakeside camp, the car park is removed from the structures. Access is by a gently curving boardwalk past a trio of vertical shafts made from tapered tree trunks collected on-site and crafted by Ian Sandmeyer of Sandmeyer Design.

RUSTIC MODERN REFINED

A house that has won raves from the design community was conceived with an interplay of inward and outward, close in and far reaching, quiet and bold. Commanding a dramatic prospect over Jackson Hole and out to the Tetons, its metaphoric inner life contemplates a natural wildflower meadow as a kind of hidden gem in nature. It's a secret garden that both inspires and grounds the homeowners every time they glimpse it. As the mountain view lifts them up and draws them out into the world, the meadow speaks to their souls.

It was the meadow, actually, that sold the property. When the owners first walked the thirty-five-acre property on the side of a ridge off the valley floor, its views were obscured by trees and dense underbrush. The owners found themselves irresistibly drawn to the beautiful natural garden, and, in a process that unfolded organically, the house was designed in response to it. It was the woman of the Connecticut-based family who insisted that the meadow be viewable from inside their home and its special nature captured. This the architects achieved. The house presents as restrained rather than monolithic. With the sheltering hillside rising behind and its Teton orientation, the structure nestles into the landscape without calling attention to itself. It was designed almost as a series of connected structures of reclaimed wood and Montana moss rock punctuated with steel and glass windows and anchored by chimneys. These articulated sections nestle into the hillside and extend on either side of a human-scaled main entry. Walking through the front door, you first experience the intimacy of the "hidden" meadow. Then, at ninety degrees, an iconic view of the Tetons

◄ A home on a ridgetop property, designed by JLF Design Build with interiors by WRJ Design, has stunning Jackson Hole views and an organic relationship to the land. The entry—human scaled, cabin-like, with double glass entry doors—is furnished with a George Nakashima credenza and suede-upholstered Holly Hunt bench. The cube chandelier is from Rocky Mountain Hardware. The bronze *Sisters (The Three Architects)* is by Albert Wein, circa 1957.

▶ A high-ceilinged room with fireplace blurs the transition from inside to out. Simple teak furniture and a large table offer both sitting and dining areas.

leads you from the entry into the heart of the house. "The entry is like a pair of arms that's open to you," explains Design Principal Paul Bertelli of JLF Design Build. "One arm is bound in the hillside. The other is a series of bedrooms that cascade down the hill. The front door is the center of the embrace. We were able to use the hillside to soften the mass of the building by bringing the sage field over it."

The JLF approach is for the design team—in this case Bertelli, JLF Principal Ashley Sullivan, and Project Manager Tyler Call—to spend extensive periods of time with the clients prior to designing a new house "to open-endedly get a feeling for what they like and don't like, or what draws them

to a particular palette," Bertelli explains. A series of concept diagrams help further the process in terms of deciding on the number, size, and relationship between rooms and the site. They then work creatively within Teton County's regulations (which address amount of glass allowed, number of wood-burning fireplaces, visibility from the valley floor, and other factors) to design a structure that is appropriate to the land and the region, that suits the family's needs, and that will last a century.

To this end JLF uses cutting-edge technologies to advance efficiencies, such as log walls and stone foundations that are as hermetically sealed as possible, in sustainable building practices. "We try to avoid nostalgia," says Bertelli. "We focus on authenticity and capture a sense of optimism about the future. What you don't see is the rigor and stoutness of this building, which has to last for a hundred years. The whole idea behind constructing a building that lasts

a century or more is that it may cost more initially or use a little more energy to produce it, but once it's done, it's done. And it's far more sustainable than much of what's being done these days. Endurance is the ultimate in sustainability."

Bertelli is quick to credit the entire team, from carpenters to stonemasons and in particular the build team of Shandon Brinkerhoff, Kenny Rasmussen, and Brady Crawford, for the success of the project, emphasizing JLF's ethos of collaboration that encourages every idea to be voiced. Designer Rush Jenkins of WRJ Interior Design worked with the homeowners to realize the interiors of the house. The clients contributed their own strong aesthetic, as well as a notable midcentury modern furniture collection and some significant art pieces.

From the simple main entry, which has the feel of a one-room homestead cabin, to the open,

◄ The great room features glass, stone, soaring ceilings, and exposed steel beams. The day bed/sofa is an Edward Wormley piece, circa 1965.

▲ The architects made the most of the drop-dead view, framing the Tetons through a floor-to-ceiling glass wall in the living room. Designer Rush Jenkins intentionally kept the palette neutral so as not to take away from the view. The coffee table is by San Francisco-based furniture designer Jiun Ho.

► The house has a carefully curated mixture of old and new pieces. The graceful Scandinavian Modern rosewood armchairs were designed by Henning Kjaernulf in the '60s.

steel-beamed living room; from an intimate glassed-in porch to the expansive kitchen with its comfortable dining area, large bank of high-efficiency windows, and white glass cabinetry; and through each bedroom, bath, and living area, the interiors balance comfort, warmth, elegance, and artistry with the dramatic scenery visible from every room.

Jenkins chose a nature-inspired palette—sage, wheat, blue—that accentuates the home's natural surroundings. He worked to introduce both coziness and a sense of grounding through weightier uphol-stered pieces and luxuriously soft accessories to counterbalance the wood floors, exposed steel, and streamlined profiles of the modern pieces. The look may be understated elegance, but a primary driving force was comfort. This is a home for an extended family and their friends and pets, for gathering together after an exhilarating day outdoors, for kick-ing back and putting up one's feet.

Once built, the building will mature over time, taking on character. The materials will weather with-out looking as if they are failing. The structure will appear even more at one with its environment. This

◄ A light-filled kitchen pushes the envelope of modern rustic, juxtaposing bright white glass cabinetry with reclaimed wood and stone. Says designer Rush Jenkins, "The glass takes on the colors surrounding it." The midcentury Dutch rosewood barstools nestle under the counter's edge when not needed, while the Lindsey Edelman chandelier makes a bold and playful statement.

▲ A separate guesthouse exhibits a related, but differ-ent, architectural vocabulary; it combines living and dining areas with a compact kitchen so guests can enjoy their own private retreat.

◄ The master bedroom suite mixes textures; a custom Elizabeth Eakins rug of gentle blue-sage tone references the colors outside. *Still Life with Black Currants* by Philip von Schantz, 1977, hangs over the custom-handcrafted bed.

▲ Master craftsmanship is displayed throughout the project, including in the his- and-her dressing areas in the master suite.

The master bath strives to not compete with the view. Individual mirrors are affixed low and can be moved. The pendants, hung at different heights, are solid glass drops illuminated by LED lights. The glass shower wall creates oneness with the outdoors.

is important, since the homeowners, who already spend half the year there and plan to move there full time, intend for the house to become the family's touchstone. Years from now, Bertelli says, when the next generation is discovering the wonders of the property and its owners realize they haven't had to replace the roof or fix the siding or paint they'll look back and realize this very intentional process was the right one.

It is a house where longevity, form, and appropriateness are as crucial as function, explains Bertelli.

"A sense of romance was important. From our perspective the vernacular should say, 'This house belongs in Jackson, Wyoming.' Architecture does contribute so much to sense of place, and our clients were clearly aligned with that philosophy. It can't just be nostalgic, though. It has to have some honesty in the twenty-first century. But, it can still have that truth within a romantic context."

▲ A quiet corner of a bedroom with built-in bookshelves and a comfortable armchair demonstrates the architects' success in giving each section of the house its privacy and still highlighting its relationship to the land.

▶ A quiet office for two, removed from the busiest part of the house, highlights the home's impeccable stone and woodwork.

RURAL
MEETS URBANE

t's unusual for an architecture firm to be offered the chance to help re-envision a family's entire life in three successive projects. But that is exactly the opportunity that was presented to Pearson Design Group by a Midwestern couple as they anticipated the empty-nest phase of their lives.

As this suburban Chicago family hit its midstream, with children having grown up and moved out of the house, the husband and wife reexamined their longtime history in the Rocky Mountains and their love of the outdoor lifestyle afforded by it. Although still working, they were no longer tethered to a particular geography or commute. Having purchased a lot in Big Sky, Montana, some years before, their first step was to conceive of a multi-phase plan for their lives going forward. They would commit incrementally, building a guesthouse first so they could experience life in Montana more fully and, while doing so, decide whether the property they'd purchased was the right one for them.

For the first phase, with the guidance of Pearson Design Group, they envisioned a structure containing guest quarters and an après-ski aerie boasting dramatic views situated atop a garage component. The resulting project offered a fresh take on traditional mountain living, with an original aesthetic finding its highest expression in the contemporary lodge-like main room of wood and glass. The couple would use the modestly scaled house as their Montana base while working through the more complicated aspects of what was really a major life change, for they intended to downsize from the family home and purchase an urban dwelling at the same time. This was complicated by the fact that they hadn't yet decided which city would be their base. After they broke ground on their main home in Montana, and after searching various cities for a pied-à-terre, they purchased an apartment in downtown Denver, within easy reach of a major airport and conveniently located near two of their children.

The Montana home was the initial focus. The property, gradually sloped, with a dense stand of lodgepole pines and strategic view corridors, allowed for plenty of natural daylight and far-reaching vistas but gave the sense of being nestled into the forest. Says Pearson Design Group architect Greg Matthews, "There's a beautiful juxtaposition of intimate wooded forest and expansive views," and the home was designed to heighten the experience. The master suite has an almost tree house–like feel, while the main living space has a large expanse of glass to take in the mountainscape. The contrast, says Matthews, "reinforces the intimacy in the private spaces and the expansive views in the public spaces."

The structure, constructed of reclaimed materials, log, and stone, would have an indigenous feel, explains the architect. "Contextually it would feel as if it were a century-old mountain lodge." It would be big enough for the extended family to gather and to entertain large groups, but was designed so that two people would feel comfortably cozy when alone. By placing the master bedroom suite in proximity to the primary living spaces, the home feels snug when the

▲ The master bedroom of a Pearson Design home at the Yellowstone Club in Montana is defined by texture. Rain Houser and Skye Anderson selected a fringed lounge chair, sheepskin rug, and fur blanket to complement the custom-designed bed and nightstands, which were commissioned through Tim Sanford. The chandelier is from John Brooks, Inc.

▶ The touchstone of the home is the custom rope swing (through Integrity Builders) that inspired the name Freedom Lodge. The swing and rope-detail chandelier convey a sense of whimsy in the great room while refined casual sofas from Urbaine Home anchor the volume. The buffalo mount is vintage, circa 1940s.

▲ An outdoor room can be enjoyed year-round thanks to the wood-burning fireplace, built-in appliances and seating, and custom-made dining table and chandelier.

▶ The entry to the Montana home celebrates the mountain modern ethos with a wall of glass and steel abutting the hand hewn log wall. Houser + Anderson chose a vintage rug, velvet wing chair, Swedish log basket, and an antique child's chair belonging to the home-owners to furnish the space. A caribou mount from the 1940s lends a sculptural grace.

◀◀ A translucent partition creates structure without closing off the staircase. At the landing, an oversized bear painting by Amy Ringholz provides a focal point.

▲ The custom bar and pool table with blackened brass pendants create a room for family fun. The art was sourced through Visions West.

◀ The custom demilune lends a feminine touch to a vestibule outside the master bedroom.

▲ A cozy nook has custom-designed sofas by Houser + Anderson and a vintage table.

▶ The generously scaled kitchen features custom cabinetry crafted by Integrity Builders and quartzite countertops and backsplash. Open shelving displays featherweight ceramic dishes from France.

◀ Extensive seating with fireside chaises and wildlife mounts provides a comfortable lounging area for the entire family.

▲ In a painted bathroom, a
floating vanity, brass accents,
and a graceful beaded chandelier lend a feminine touch.

▶ A sculptural carved marble
tub makes a dramatic statement in a master bath with
custom vanities and mirrors.

▲ Houser + Anderson designed the bed and finished the room with an angular chandelier and textural rug.

▶ The bunk room features beds made from oak timbers, industrial pipe-fitting hand rails, and a vintage Moroccan rug.

▲ A soft color palette, carved headboard, and over-scaled paper flower pendant create an eclectic guest room aesthetic. The Moroccan pom-pom blanket and alpaca rug add texture while the gilded European elk mount injects an unexpected touch of rustic glam.

▲ The functional workspace is finished with a custom-designed desk, vintage rug, and Verellen sofa.

▲ A feminine office with pinks and blues features a vintage rug and a chandelier made of agate.

couple is in residence but effortlessly expands for a crowd when the family gathers. Although many Big Sky homes are designed with the winter experience in mind, this makes the most of outdoor living, with easy access to the yard and the outdoor dining/living area. The open-air room has a wrap-around bench and fireplace incorporated into its design, and a large dining table, built-in grill, and cooking facilities for outdoor dining in all seasons.

The home celebrates local materials where possible while incorporating steel and other contemporary touches—a semi-transparent glass partition along the base of the stairs, a rope chandelier and swing in the living room, cool steel piping and plates for railings and steps in the bunk room. "They wanted something lighter, brighter, and a little more light-hearted," says interior designer Rain Houser, who collaborated with Skye Anderson in working with the couple on all three projects over

a five-year period. "They wanted a house that portrayed their personalities."

Successfully crafting a home that fits in such a rugged environment while still conveying a contemporary spirit, says Matthews, requires a thoughtful process. Their success lay in staying true to traditional forms but striving to apply some modern concepts while creating something playful and unique.

As the mountain home took shape, the Denver apartment, for use primarily during the shoulder seasons and as a convenient launching pad for work-related travel, was to be a true pied-à-terre, designed to fulfill the couple's needs rather than accommodate a family. In contrast to the mountain home, the urban loft would be compact, its style more contemporary, with some rustic touches in a nod to the mile-high mountain locale. Most unusual for city living, it would celebrate an indoor/outdoor

ethos via an open rooftop living area that accesses a guest room casita and office.

Located close to restaurants, cultural opportunities, and mass transit, the apartment was perfect in theory but stark and unwelcoming in real life. "It was a builder's box, with less than desirable finishes at first glance," recalls designer Rain Houser. Asked to complete the job quickly, she created a foyer-like area by placing a screen made of live-edge walnut slabs between the elevator and living room, applied grass cloth to cover the dark tones on existing columns, installed motorized shades for privacy and a live-edge-topped bar for character, and worked to incorporate the clients' antiques from their home in Illinois. Houser and her clients turned a small existing office into a bar area, warmed the spaces using tones that were compatible with existing materials, infused varied textures, and added some sculptural pieces with character in order to create a cozier, more home-like and welcoming feel while still tapping into the energy of city living.

The result is a clean, fresh, stylish oasis of calm in the heart of a dynamic city. The Montana dwelling, in contrast, "is fresh but timeless, with one foot in traditional roots and one in a modern lifestyle," according to Matthews. Together, the two homes—one small, one large; one city, one country; one modern with rustic details, one rustic with modern details—provide the perfect juxtaposition for a couple embracing their next phase of life with passion, with clear-eyed vision, and with an unbounded love of the West.

◄ The interiors of a Denver pied-à-terre were updated by Houser + Anderson for turnkey city living.

▲ A rooftop terrace with sculptural lounge chairs and comfortable sectionals becomes the ultimate refuge in the heart of the city.

▶ Vintage leather club chairs offer the perfect spot to relax in the glass-walled office/ casita accessed from the rooftop terrace.

◄ An ochre chandelier hovers above a round McGuire dining table; the equine photography by Tracie Spence makes a dramatic statement and serves as a reminder of the apartment's place in the West.

▲ The kitchen is brightened by white cabinetry and countertops and an artistic pendant array.

▶ A mirror installation hangs above the clients' vintage chairs. An antique book press adds interest to the space.

◄ The designers created an opening in what had originally been a small office and installed a live-edge slab as a bar top to expand the entertaining possibilities of the suite of rooms.

► A down sofa, fur throw, organic coffee table, and textured details create a cozy den.

► Serenity was the goal in this urban master bedroom. Soft fabrics and tones with organic bedside tables, a plush lounge chair and wool drapes transform the room into a true retreat.

CONTEMPORARY ADOBE

Although it is true that exciting, cutting-edge design can result from a process of jousting personalities and strong opinions, in a home designed for an art-centered, restorative phase of life after a long professional career, harmony suits.

When a corporate CEO in Kansas decided to build a home in anticipation of her retirement to Santa Fe, she chose her team wisely. Each was a seasoned veteran in his field: Larry Andren in architecture, David Naylor in interior design, and Kim Dressel of Dressel Construction in building fine homes. She articulated her needs and her aesthetic, introduced them to her artwork, and agreed to a plan and schedule. Then, while remaining available for consultation, she trusted the team to execute the vision.

She was not coming in cold. The client had a deeply felt personal history in the region; she was a longtime visitor to Santa Fe who had amassed a significant collection of regional art. She already knew Larry Andren, an iconic architect at the twilight of his professional career who had moved to the Southwest three decades previously upon receiving his architecture degree from Montana State University. After designing seventy-five homes over eleven years in the Scottsdale area, Andren relocated to Santa Fe, where, over the course of twenty years and another eighty homes, he perfected a calm, creative discipline that has served his clients well in balancing programmatic needs with a wide range of restrictive design guidelines in Santa Fe.

In this project, Andren was involved from the very beginning; he even helped the client select her site, the first step in a successful collaboration. "The site is really so important," Andren attests. "It contributes so much to the design."

The design process began with equal consideration given to the landscape and the client's expressed needs. The steeply sloped, piñon- and juniper-covered lot is north of town, outside the most strictly curtailed historic areas (Santa Fe has seventeen), but still subject to city requirements (such as building to

◄ The late architect Larry Andren and designer David Naylor collaborated on an art-filled home in Santa Fe for a busy CEO and collector. Naylor chose tones to match the Tony Abeyta triptych and pieces that wouldn't compete with either the art or the views. The teak coffee table matches the shape of the curved sofa. Naylor designed it with a sizable niche to lighten its mass and provide space for a remote or stack of magazines.

▶ Terrace furniture has clean, curving lines. A fountain sourced from Stone Forest in Santa Fe enhances the sensation of being outdoors in nature.

LEED-certification standards). Its location in a well-planned subdivision brought additional restrictive covenants. Height, color, and material choices were limited, while county stipulations such as water-retention ponds for permanent erosion control had to be met.

The downhill nature of the prospect proscribed solar collectors on the rooftop for aesthetic reasons. Andren had to work creatively to meet the LEED certification requirements in other ways, such as using sophisticated ventilation systems. Although designing to such standards can take longer, cost more and limit creativity, Andren says, "It makes for compatible subdivisions, much to the frustration of some architects who might want to spread their wings. But these guidelines we complain about are the reason so many people come here for vacations and end up moving here. It has worked very well."

After four to five months of drawing, and close consultation with the client as well as interior designer David Naylor, another luminary in the Santa Fe design community who was brought on to the team early, Andren says the end result is very near the original concept. The home—a 3,000-square-foot,

two-bedroom structure with a study, media room, and exercise room—is wood-framed, with a three-coat cement stucco exterior and three-coat plaster interior, giving it the warmth, organic feel, and soft curves of a true adobe. The entire structure is built into the hillside and oriented toward expansive views of the Sangre de Cristo Mountains. An intimately scaled entry, accessed from the street, or barrier, side, is grounded by a massive bench-like block of granite, a stone-and-river-rock water feature and a dramatic art piece in the form of a pivoting glass and steel door (designed by David Naylor and fabricated locally). Upon entering, the space opens up and extends across the living room, with its curved seating area, highly refined finishes and striking art collection, to a multilevel patio with spectacular mountain views.

▲ Detail of a contemporary painting by Navajo artist Tony Abeyta reveals the complexity and depth of his mixed media works, which are inspired by New Mexico's landscape and history.

▶ A carefully composed bedroom features the owner's art—including a painting by John Gary Brown over the headboard—and a silk-and-wool rug in complementary colors.

The client's artwork collection—mainly Southwestern paintings and contemporary ceramics and glass collected in the Midwest—existed prior to the house. The pieces were photographed and sized as the design process began, with Naylor working to place the largest paintings, by Navajo mixed-media artist Tony Abeyta, and designing live-edge wood display shelving and niches for the sculptural ceramic and glass vessels. The client knew and was able to express the style she was seeking, says Naylor. "We knew the art was the feature, so all the rugs and fixtures supported that. She wanted contemporary pieces that were very clean and monochromatic. We wanted to create the bass notes, because we knew the artwork was going to provide the visual high notes. It was so great to have a collection that was so well curated, timely, and regional."

The homeowner had collected art and craft pieces over the previous thirty years, always with a retirement home in the West in mind. She discovered the work of Tony Abeyta through a Kansas art dealer who advised her to look at his work when she visited Santa Fe. "I have no expertise," she says. "I just know what I like, and I like art that me makes me look over and over again and find something new."

Naylor selected statement lighting, sleek chrome and stainless steel kitchen and bathroom accessories, and unusual artisan tile selections that experiment with texture and scale. He would lay out choices in order of preference and in virtually every case the owner's selection aligned with the team's. By the end of the project, the designers relate, the team was so attuned that the process flowed organically in an intuitive, deeply realized, organized, and organic series of decisions. "We were speaking shorthand by then," Naylor says. "There was a lot of trust and faith because the house was very understood."

For instance, when a German porcelain tile they'd chosen for the main living areas arrived it was

The master bath is filled with the same light and views that make New Mexico a mecca for artists. Floating vanities, white vessel sinks, and a rectilinear white bathtub keep the minimalist interiors light and airy.

◄ Contemporary stainless steel fixtures and clean surfaces characterize a kitchen where much of the wall space has been given over to windows. "You just don't want to compete with the view," says designer David Naylor. The organic tones of the wood counter chairs add warmth to the relatively austere space.

▶ The house gets its biggest jolt of color from three abstract artworks by mixed-media painter Craig A. Hetler. The light fixture is by Hubbardton Forge.

▲ A glimpse of the bedroom rug reveals a palette chosen to complement the owner's art pieces and reflect the colors of the sky.

▶ In a bathroom, a trio of handblown hanging glass light fixtures were chosen so as not to interfere with the organic tile and wood slab countertop. A remnant of the live-edge wood slab was used as a partial shelf beneath.

▶ ▶ Live-edge cantilevered shelves in the living room display the owner's collection of art glass pieces collected mostly in the Midwest.

◄◄ The entry courtyard conveys the appropriate sense of arrival with a massive granite bench and a dramatic, custom-made oversized pivoting door designed by David Naylor.

◄ The Zen-like water feature provides natural sounds that ease the transition from the nearby road and parking area to the interior of the home.

markedly different from the sample they'd seen; it was more active, with greater contrast. Naylor laid eight tiles down and found he liked the activity. He visualized the finished house and made the decision that the flooring would work well with the client's pottery collection, a bold move he only would have made because of the client's "artistic acceptance" and the fact that he knew she loved organic, interesting tile. In the end it was a fortuitous accident that helped marry the house to the art.

Recently retired and relocated, the homeowner is now ensconced in a home that looks to and celebrates the land while being grounded in its artistic expression. Says Andren, "It's a neat house in that

it expresses the personality of its owner and really addresses the site: the slopes, the vegetation, the climactic considerations, the views. When you stand in the house, the views are right in your face. It's overwhelming. And," he adds, "it's only about five minutes to the Plaza."

Artistic affinity and professional trust between the designers, the builder, and the client constituted the starting and end point of a project characterized throughout by harmony. "We were pushed outside our comfort zone," reflects David Naylor, "but not outside our intellectual abilities." The house represents the best efforts of a talented team: it makes a bold artistic statement, yet still feels like home.

GLASS & STONE HOMESTEAD

An iconic refuge for rusticators over the past century, Jackson Hole is populated with an eclectic array of architecture: log cabins, midcentury ranch homes, reclaimed timber structures, renovated barns, funky alternative dwellings, and modernist glass aeries. Each in its way is a fitting expression of the western experience and an appropriate response to one of the world's most spectacular natural settings. Indeed, it is almost impossible to build in the area without the scenery constituting one of the most important voices in the dialogue. But there *is* a dialogue, one that takes place between the designers, the owners, and the setting. And the most successful architecture—appropriate, original, beautiful, and soulful—gives equal weight to all three constituents. It occupies that space where scenery offers inspiration and regionalism provides the palette, but where form and function marry in an original and personal vision.

The creative forces at JLF Design Build are masters of regional vernacular expression. The firm is known for original place-based architecture imbued with a sense of permanence and handcraftedness. Wyoming-based interior designer Tayloe Piggott works closely with clients throughout an intensive process whose end result is a home that reflects their personality, lifestyle, and needs. According to Piggott and JLF's Paul Bertelli, a new home on an elevated site with spectacular views was the direct result of a harmonious meeting of sensibilities. While the clients had a distinct vision to articulate, they allowed themselves to be guided by the design professionals. Throughout the process, all parties were

stretched to consider new approaches while working collaboratively. The end result is a home that serves its purpose perfectly as a vacation retreat for a frequently relocating dual-career British-American family. Ultimately, it will readily adapt to become the family's full-time residence.

The family was relatively new to Jackson Hole, but they all fell hard for it on their first visit. Once they found their perfect property—one that extends from sagebrush flats to timbered foothills and is favored by moose and elk—it didn't take them long to alight on the work of JLF Design Build. They loved the JLF homes they saw and knew that their home would be carefully crafted, built to last, and designed for them in a very personal way.

The clients were living in England during the design process. There they had been strongly influenced by the serene solidity of eighteenth- and nineteenth-century stone farm buildings found throughout the Cotswold Hills. The concept, explains Bertelli, was to build a more compact house with a modernist take and less obvious western detailing that would take full advantage of the scenery. "The inspiration for all the stone came from that vision [of homes in the Cotswolds]," says Bertelli. "Normally we might add more western typography, but the all-stone building was built out of that sensibility, and the clients' relationship with England."

The three-story structure is built into the hillside and oriented toward a panorama of the Tetons. "It is not ornate or grand in any way," says Bertelli, "but it has spectacular views." Conceived as two structural masses with a striking glass dining room serving as the functional connective element, it is simultaneously rustic and modern. It is rugged enough to stand up to the site and the weather, and simple enough to not compete with the views. It cleverly incorporates modernist elements: large, unbroken expanses of glass; a metal roof; clean lines; minimal decorative details; and a stunning glass staircase. The staircase makes a dramatic sculptural statement. It also serves as a lightwell for the entire structure, conveying sunlight from the skylight above to the boys' rooms on the lowest floor.

"The original vision was to have something timeless that wouldn't date itself over the next few decades," the owners explain. "We wanted rustic but modern, something very much in keeping with Jackson and the surroundings that would blend the views and the look and feel of the property. We

A waterfall-like chandelier and minimally profiled dining chairs do little to impede the view through the dining room to the Tetons. The patio is furnished with restraint; the cedar living chairs were purchased through Almond Hartzog in San Francisco.

◄◄ A quiet corner celebrates the texture of wood floors and stone walls with natural light. The homeowners' history in South America and Europe is reflected in their mostly Latin American art collection and international choice of fabrics, here from Osborne & Little (English) and Manuel Canovas (French).

◄ The dining room serves as a connective element between the two main structures of the house. It is minimally furnished with scissor back chairs of Italian rosewood, circa 1960, and Ochre's drizzle chandelier of clear glass drops cascading from a polished nickel frame.

A precision-engineered glass staircase makes a dramatic architectural statement while serving as a "lightwell." It conveys daylight through the house to the bedrooms on the lowest floor.

wanted stone, a lot of glass to take advantage of the views, and old wood—oak, not cherry."

The goal, says Bertelli, was "to bring a different contrasting edge to the regional context."

Rooms are kept simple with stone walls and wood ceilings and floors. The owners chose unfussy furniture and airy light fixtures. According to Tayloe Piggott, the clients brought much to the conversation in terms of an interior palette, again influenced by their personal history in English country houses. Fabrics that pop—such as bold, large-scale floral patterns on wing chairs by the fireplace—inject life, color, and an unexpected playfulness into living spaces. The kitchen and bathrooms, designed by JLF Design Build, display the most contemporary expressions; modern-leaning cabinets and fixtures and a stunning glass tile backsplash in the sleek-surfaced kitchen are offset by rustic ceilings.

The interiors have verve, but they also show restraint. Says Piggott, "I really believe less is more in a home such as this, because the beautiful architecture is the voice that wants to be heard in the home."

The house *is* beautiful, and respectful of the environment. But the proof is in the function, in the way the home fulfills its occupants. In this regard it is beyond successful. The homeowners, who have since moved from England to New York to Miami, have found that the home offers a much needed respite and sense of quietude for a peripatetic family. It meets all their needs, whether they're hosting friends and family or sipping a cup of tea while looking out at the Grand Teton on a wintry morning. And they look forward to the day it becomes their primary residence.

"This was an exciting project," says Bertelli. "We were challenged to go in a different direction and didn't know how far we could take it, but the clients said, 'Show us what's possible.' In that environment, you're more relaxed and more willing to take risks. Their motivation was their love of the place and their love of their boys, and the desire for a place of sanctuary and respite. A lot of people are motivated by different things," he adds, "but they were driven by a respect for the West and a respect for the area." That respect is evident in a home that is rooted in the landscape, yet still inspired by the broader world.

▲ Glass tiles required the utmost care in installation but infuse the space with color and give the rustic kitchen a modernist edge.

▶ Sleek countertops, flat-fronted cabinetry, steel details, and Olly counter stools combine with the sage green backsplash and built-in window seat to marry rustic and modern elements in a kitchen designed to be a comfortable spot for the family to gather.

◄ Wide floorboards and wood details lend a farmhouse feel to the upstairs rooms. The bedroom celebrates clean lines in its velvet upholstered headboard, Codor Design nightstand, and wall sconce by Marian Jamieson. The custom bedding fabric is from Pollack. The owner prefers to go rug free, the better to enjoy the character of the old floorboards.

▲ The home's bathrooms lean industrial contemporary, with translucent glass panels, apothecary-style cabinets, and large, unadorned windows.

◀ English wing chairs provide comfortable seating and an unexpected pop of color in Manuel Canovas floral fabric. The large mirror by Ochre brings light into the stone room and reflects the simple lines of the chandelier. The rounded seating arranged around a Tuell & Reynolds table encourages intimate conversations around the hearth.

FARMHOUSE REINVENTED

When choosing where to build, Montana's early home-steaders were driven by practical reasons. They were less interested in maximizing their views than in seeking relief from the elements and having access to water—two essential considerations in such an arid and windswept land-scape. When a couple from Louisiana, passionate about fly-fishing and motivated to tread lightly on the land, purchased a run-down homestead property with more than a mile of Yellowstone River frontage, they took their cues from their forebears. Although the parcel is large, the home is small. Although there are expansive views from the property's upper reaches, they sited down low, in the relative shelter of mature trees. As the original owner did, they built close to the river. And when it came to design, they worked with their architectural team to envision a structure inspired by its agricultural heritage and appropriate to the landscape.

"Size was something I cared about," explains owner Tom Gattle. "Everyone wants to build these big buildings, but I didn't want that. I wanted to keep it under 2,000 square feet of heated area. The property could handle anything, but this is a place to hike, fish, and enjoy the West. We built for a more intimate experience."

Architect Reid Smith proposed the notion of a modern farmhouse for contemporary Montana living, one that brings the outdoors in but refers in

▲ The kitchen of a modern farmhouse on a private mile of the Yellowstone River has an open plan that makes the most of natural light. Backless seating, glass globes, white under-counter cabinetry, and open shelving help maintain a feel of airiness. The metal on the vent hood and island countertop is repurposed.

▶ The entry, kitchen, and living room flow together. Although the house is small at under 2,000 square feet, architect Reid Smith designed it to comfortably expand to accommodate several couples at once. Stained white oak floors throughout the public rooms help unify the space.

◄ The front door with windows leans modern while allowing in light and maintaining a connection to the outdoors. The custom abstract painting by Michigan artist Becca Schlaff speaks to the owner's passion for fishing and his motivation for enhancing the free-flowing water systems and fishery on the 220-acre property.

► The home's outdoor space was cleverly designed within its building footprint for protection from the wind and to command views of the mountain landscape and river frontage.

structure to its agricultural heritage. The house is actually composed of two architectural forms: a traditional gabled primary building and a more contemporary shed-roofed additive structure, both anchored by one large chimney. A covered outdoor room oriented toward the river extends the living space without thrusting into the landscape. In an area known for its winds, the designers pulled the outdoor living space out of the prevailing breezes but positioned it so that one can still hear the rapids and see down river. "We created an acoustic scoop that gathers the sounds from the river," says Reid Smith, "and took the opportunity to use architecture to capitalize on the existing natural features."

In its placement (in proximity to the original homestead and nestled up against a giant ancient willow tree), and in its use of ranch vernacular, "the whole project was a show of respect and a recognition of history, a time when things were kept simple and life was connected to the landscape," says project architect Bob Brooks.

Once square footage and basic form had been agreed upon, Tom Gattle left the design process in the capable hands of the architects and his wife, Edna, who gathered input from a number of designers for various elements of the finished interiors. The idea behind the structure was to be as appropriate in, aware of, and open to the outside as possible. Galvanized metal, wood, and stone help the house blend into the landscape, while its restrained size (1,900 square feet, with three bedrooms and three baths) forces the attention outside. Size also drove the decision to create contemporary-leaning interiors. "I wanted to make the best use of that space," says Edna Gattle. "I thought going with a more modern rustic look would make the house feel larger and less closed in while remaining true to Montana. And it's such a beautiful area, I wanted the inside to reflect the outside as far as colors, stone, and materials used. Whether you're looking at the water or the Crazy Mountains, I wanted it all to work together."

While his wife was selecting finishes and furnishings, Gattle turned his attention to his real passion, which was the land, the river, and the fishery. A lifelong fly-fisherman who has traveled the world in pursuit of the sport, he had been fishing the Yellowstone for years. It was their son who found the 220-acre property—a triangular piece, with the longest side an entire mile of the river—for sale

◄ A quiet twin room makes clever use of reclaimed fir planks affixed to the wall as mock headboards. Connie Howard of Woodvale Interiors in Louisiana suggested the whimsical treatment.

► A bedroom's subdued palette of cream and gray creates a serene retreat for guests. Many of the small accessories throughout the house were sourced by the owner through Catherine Lane Interiors in Livingston, Montana.

online and showed it to his parents. Gattle had actually fished through the property a number of times and he had an idea about what he wanted to do.

The team tore down the existing dilapidated buildings and built a simple infrastructure: a road that conveys visitors from the public road across the bench then down to the riverside, and an extension to the road that runs along the length of the property for access to the river from both ends. They did some work to shore up sections of the riverbank that were being washed away and applied for and received a permit to develop a spring creek, since there are several that flow from the bench year-round. The previous owner had channeled the flow of water, Gattle explains. "I decided to undo that and allow it to flow through the lower areas. The water will be redirected and create an environment that will allow fish to come up and spawn, and it will become a part of the river system itself."

The site has a native landscape of grasslands and cottonwoods, which is kept natural right up to the edge of the house. The views of the Crazy Mountains from the upper portions of the property are stunning, but are also expansive from the lowland portion. The river, of course, is the source of life. "In normal summer flow, the river has a lot of character, a lot of riffles," Gattle says. "It's a beautiful section of the river."

◄ The master bedroom is kept small, relatively un-accessorized, and deliberately monochromatic so as not to compete with the views.

▲ A floating vanity, unframed mirrors, open shelves, and white vessel sinks atop a wood slab countertop extend the theme of simplicity and airiness.

A marshy area on the property attracts waterfowl; wildlife is abundant throughout. "It's been such a pleasant surprise," says Edna Gattle. "We've had eagles on our property, and in the spring, turkeys strutting across the river. In the evening six or seven mule deer will walk between the house and the water. There are egrets, too. It feels like our very own nature preserve."

The architects at Reid Smith are proud of an understated, human-scaled design that celebrates the land and its history. "We've captured both the old and the new," says Reid Smith. "I guess you could say it captures both centuries."

▶ A sliding door which is covered in a custom patina metal and moves on a galvanized steel box track, provides a rustic modern edge. The architect suggested it as a way of bringing a ranch-like feeling inside the house.

▶▶ Architect Reid Smith designed the modestly scaled modern farmhouse sited along a mile of the Yellowstone River to sit lightly on the land while referencing the property's agricultural past and ranching environs.

▼ The frontier sandstone fireplace, wood slab mantel, weighty furniture, and built-in seating anchor the interior space in a room given over to large windows and the expansive view.

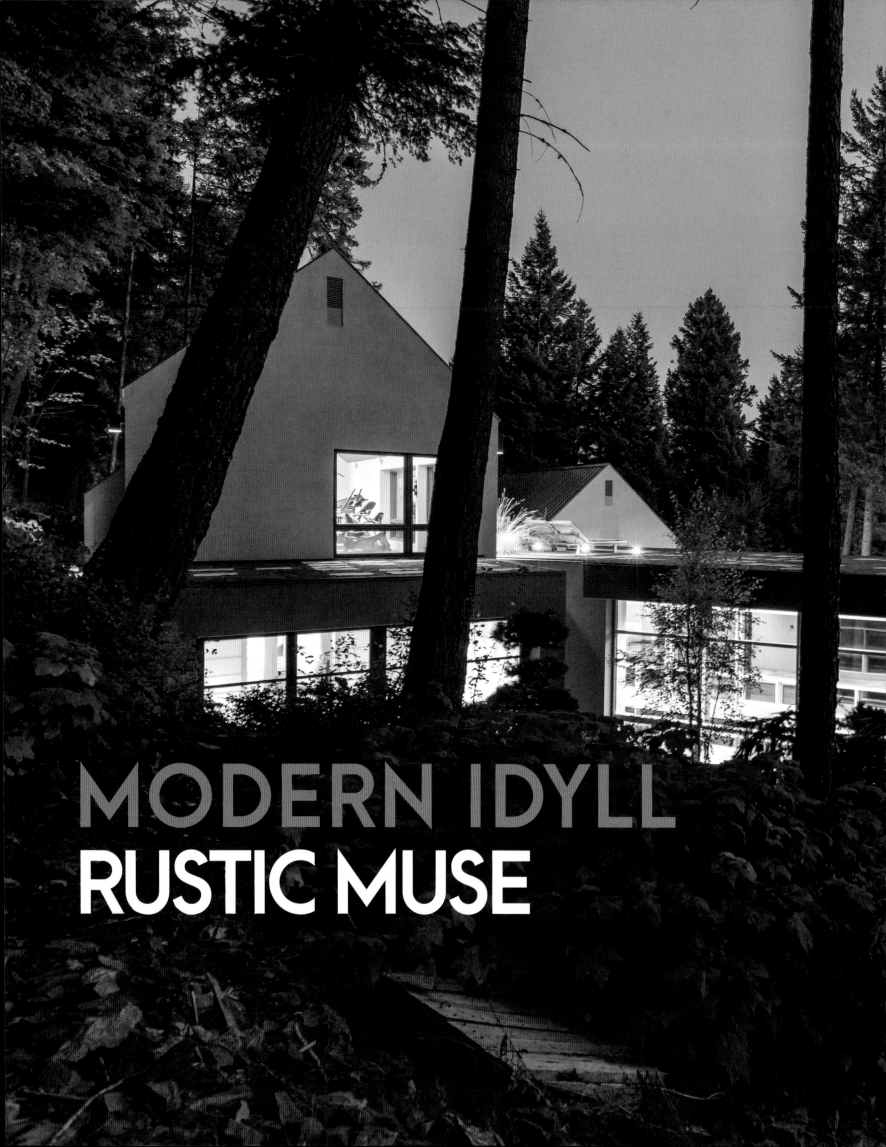

MODERN IDYLL
RUSTIC MUSE

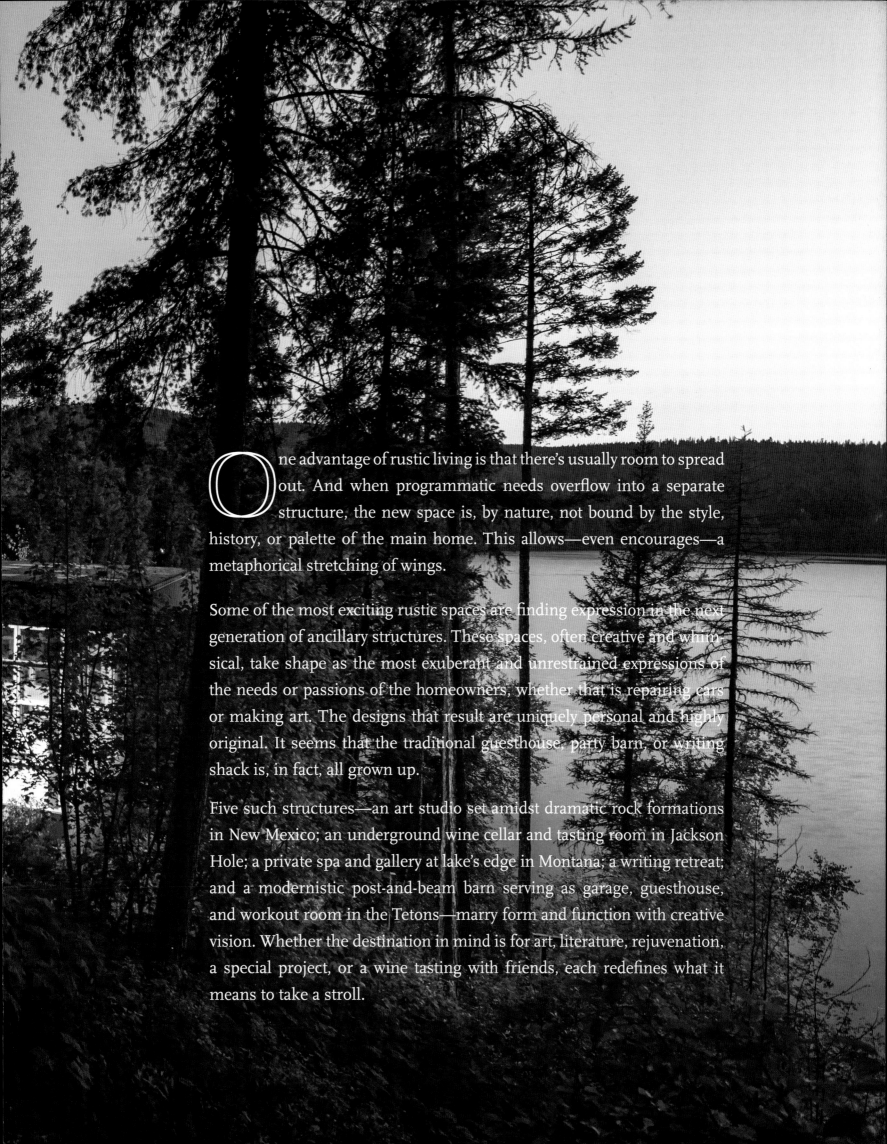

One advantage of rustic living is that there's usually room to spread out. And when programmatic needs overflow into a separate structure, the new space is, by nature, not bound by the style, history, or palette of the main home. This allows—even encourages—a metaphorical stretching of wings.

Some of the most exciting rustic spaces are finding expression in the next generation of ancillary structures. These spaces, often creative and whimsical, take shape as the most exuberant and unrestrained expressions of the needs or passions of the homeowners, whether that is repairing cars or making art. The designs that result are uniquely personal and highly original. It seems that the traditional guesthouse, party barn, or writing shack is, in fact, all grown up.

Five such structures—an art studio set amidst dramatic rock formations in New Mexico; an underground wine cellar and tasting room in Jackson Hole; a private spa and gallery at lake's edge in Montana; a writing retreat; and a modernistic post-and-beam barn serving as garage, guesthouse, and workout room in the Tetons—marry form and function with creative vision. Whether the destination in mind is for art, literature, rejuvenation, a special project, or a wine tasting with friends, each redefines what it means to take a stroll.

SLOPESIDE WINE CELLAR

rchitectural projects have a way of taking on lives of their own, especially when creative minds come together to create a synergy that the individuals involved could never have foreseen. A beautifully crafted and remarkably engineered hidden wine cellar on the mountain at Teton Village proves that anything is possible, given passion, ingenuity, and an open mind.

The young Bay Area family loved their ski vacations in Jackson Hole but had outgrown their Teton Village home. They purchased a larger existing home closer to the slopes and found that, although it had more than enough room, there was nowhere to store the wine the owners collected. The original proposal, architect Kevin Burke recalls, was to find a way to create storage for perhaps 500 bottles, most likely in a corner of the existing basement. At the time, Burke, a partner of the firm Carney Logan Burke Architects, had a full slate and not much bandwidth for what sounded like a very small project, but he went with an open mind to meet with the caretaker and view the house and ascertain its possibilities.

The house was large but severely constricted by a small site with steep grade changes. There was a partial basement, but there wasn't a lot of room to work with. The project appeared to be a modest renovation. Once Burke met with the owner, however, things got more complicated—and significantly more inspired. Together they assessed the owner's needs (500 bottles was just not going to do it), and together they started getting very creative indeed. The owner proposed a larger project accommodating closer to 1,000 bottles, as well as a tasting area, but because of county size restrictions there was nowhere to go but below grade. The most obvious thought was to expand the basement, but the technological challenges inherent in that were prohibitive. It was then that Burke suggested excavating below the driveway and parking area.

Previous page An ultra-modern subterranean wine cellar proved an engineering feat for Carney Logan Burke Architects and Dembergh Construction but the end result, tucked under the driveway, cleverly integrates into the slope-side site.

▲ The project grew from a small storage space in an existing basement to a state-of-the-art cellar with storage for 7,500 bottles of wine. The wine racks and stainless steel cabinets were designed by the architect and manufactured by Spearhead Timberworks in British Columbia.

Instead of telling him he was crazy, Burke recalls, the owner simply asked, "What would that look like?"

Many late-night design sessions, complicated engineering discussions, and countless hours later, the result is a 2,500-square-foot underground suite with climate-controlled storage for 7,500 bottles, a powder room, wet bar/kitchenette, and a sculptural lounge space with a dramatic curved ceiling. The very contemporary aesthetic celebrated there stands in decided contrast to the home's more traditional mountain design; the two distinct spaces are joined by a stairway passage whose materials suggest a transition but hardly prepare the visitor for the surprise that is in store eighteen feet below. In fact, any visitors approaching the house (walking from the guest

parking area along the driveway, then through a carefully calibrated landscape of plantings, walkways, and a bridge over a waterfall to the front door) would have no hint that they were walking across the top of a luxurious subterranean hideaway.

The project was not without its complications, says Burke. "It became one of the most technologically challenging projects we have ever had to work with. We essentially blew up the driveway, eliminating access for all construction activities. Then we found we had an underground spring, and that the snowmelt from the resort's nearby slopes runs under the house and driveway. Two walls of this project are adjacent to the garage, so how do you dig down eighteen feet and not undermine the footings of the garage? Then, once we were through all the

Comfortable modernistic furniture for lounging and a formal table (crafted by Brandner Design in Bozeman, along with blackened steel doors) for tastings are all that's needed in a room where the architecture makes a grand statement.

gymnastics of engineering the existing house from falling into the excavation holes, we had to create a watertight concrete box that could withstand a stream and the weight of a fire truck parked on top."

With help from the creative minds at Spearhead Timberworks, which prefabricated all the wood and helped design a curved ceiling that could conceal the complex ductwork, and Dembergh Construction of Jackson Hole, the addition surprises, delights, and more than fulfills its promise. From a hallway off the main public spaces of the house, a stone stairway with mahogany walls and a flowing, recessed, blackened steel handrail leads the visitor downstairs and opens into a room of wood, stone, glass, and minimal modernist furnishings. Wall-to-wall south-facing windows

admit natural light and open up to a view of water, boulders, and a steep treed slope; a glass door can be opened for access to a modestly scaled patio. Beyond a sheer glass wall with a cleverly designed retractable curtain stand rows and rows of custom-designed shelving filled with bottles. The smooth, curved ceiling creates a sense of luxury, intimacy, and cave-like shelter. There's a feeling of timelessness in the space that perfectly promotes its goal: to enjoy fine wines with the best of friends.

To be involved with such a project was a gift for its designers. The project may have started as a simple retrofit of a basement corner, but, says Burke, "At the end of the day, the client gave us creative license to do something really special."

▲ A blackened steel handrail recessed in a mahogany wall guides the visitor down a textural stone staircase from main house to wine cave.

▲ The project involved clever management of an underground stream as well as mountain runoff. The wine cellar opens to a patio and the sound of running water.

Minimal furnishings highlight the quality of the project's materials and craftsmanship.

INSPIRED
BY ART

N ew Mexico's Turquoise Trail is as evocative in real life as the promise in its name. Beginning in the Cibola National Forest just outside Albuquerque, traversing the 10,600-foot Sandia Crest and culminating in the Galisteo Basin just south of Santa Fe, the sixty-five-mile route passes through historic villages and otherworldly scenery. At its northern end, the trail—part of El Camino Real de Tierra Adentro, the original King's Road from Mexico City during colonial times—is defined by an area of striking rock formations, dubbed the "Little Garden of the Gods" by surveyors in the 1800s.

This unique landscape, with its distinctly sculptural forms set against the ever-expansive New Mexican sky, resonated deeply with sculptor Kevin Box when he first saw it in 2006. The quality of the light, the tangible sense of history (the site is a mile from one of the largest pueblos ever excavated and two miles from one of the oldest prehistoric turquoise mines in North America), and, above all, the dramatic natural formations made it the perfect place to create art.

A printmaker and graphic artist turned sculptor, Box at the time had ambitious plans to establish a nonprofit organization that would build a museum and sculpture garden with studios and living quarters for resident artists. Empowered by the willingness of the Frank Lloyd Wright School of Architecture to undertake the creation of a master plan as a professional project for its students, Box and his new wife, Jennifer, were only somewhat daunted by the project's eleven-million-dollar price tag. Between 2008 and 2010, however, as

▲ The whimsical origami-in-spired artworks by Sculptor Kevin Box and his wife Jennifer are on display to the public at their combination gallery, studio, and home south of Santa Fe. The live/work structure lies along New Mexico's Turquoise Trail and adjacent to the Garden of the Gods, so named for its monu-mental natural rock garden.

▶ Originally conceived as a nonprofit museum and art school, the structure was designed to be versatile so that the home, tucked behind the gallery/studio, can one day be turned into live/work spaces for emerging and established artists. The Frank Lloyd Wright School of Architecture worked with Box in designing the project; Box says it's like living in a sculpture.

▸The display spaces are serene and simple and benefit from copious amounts of natural light.

▸▸ The studio has a garage door and generous covered area so that the sculptor can easily wheel large works in and out of the studio, and so that he can work outside year-round.

the master plan took shape and Box attempted to raise money and secure planning permission from the county, the economy slowed drastically. In the meantime, his own career took off, so much so that Jennifer quit her job to work with Kevin full time. In addition, they were outgrowing their existing work space. It was a perceptive county planner who suggested they build in stages. They could acquire the funding and permission for a home and studio complex for their own live/work needs, while viewing it as merely a stage of evolution in the larger master plan.

The plan produced by the Frank Lloyd Wright School of Architecture consisted of a detailed report, a scale model, and a large display that was unveiled to the public at a professional conference and also exhibited at Taliesin West. It addressed specifics in locations, siting, and architectural style, and proposed green building materials and techniques best suited to the region's environment and landscape.

The 3,800-square-foot two-part structure was designed by Box, with architectural plans drawn by Alexander Dzurec of Autotroph Architecture. Box's design places the entry to the public spaces and studio, gallery, reception, and workshop up front,

closest to the road, car park, and sculpture garden, which is open to the public seasonally. The residence lies behind, connected by a twelve-by-twenty-foot breezeway, which was the suggestion of Victor Sidy, former dean of the Frank Lloyd Wright School of Architecture. The breezeway links the spaces but creates separation; it also creates a much needed and well utilized outdoor room by providing additional living space. The residence's sense of privacy is enhanced by its strategic placement between two twenty-five-foot-tall natural rock outcroppings. Both structures are two stories; the studio's second story is used as an upstairs office, while the second floor of the house has a loft space and living area for the master bedroom suite.

The master planning process introduced Box to principles of green building techniques. The school's recommendation was to build a LEED-certified building. "This was all very new to me," Box recalls. "I was just an artist at this point, and it was a steep learning curve. But the reality today is that you can do efficient designs and can make it low cost and low maintenance over the long haul."

The Box home and studio is all electric and uses ground-source heat pump technology, also known

as geoexchange, to heat and cool the structures by running water through floors and radiators. A 9.8 kilowatt array of photovoltaic panels on the roof generates more electricity than needed to power LED lights and appliances. Careful window placement and shade design maximize heat in the winter while minimizing its effects in the summer. The property is blessed with an artesian spring, frequented by Native Americans for thousands of years.

The aesthetic suggested by the School of Architecture combines a minimalist interior with a clean, monochromatic palette with dry stack stone walls inside and outside the buildings. Says Box, "It's Chaco Canyon meets midcentury modern. The dry stack walls are a historic homage to Native Americans. The rest is done in corrugated steel, compressed concrete, and Hardy board, with shed-style metal roofs."

Although the region's typical style is adobe, Box points out that traditional mud bricks and flat roofs are relatively high maintenance, with the modern adobe-look versions even more prone to cracking

stucco, leaking roofs, and melting mud bricks. In contrast, even at an altitude of 6,000 feet, with 10 percent average humidity and very high UV exposure, an exterior of concrete, stone, and steel means no cracking and no maintenance. "It makes a difference in the long run," Box observes, "if you're building a hundred-year building."

And Box is nothing if not focused on the long run. Just as he switched media early in his career from printmaking and graphic design to the more lasting medium of cast bronze, so his architectural legacy is meant to endure for the ages.

"From the beginning," explains Box, "it was engineered and designed to someday be re-commissioned as a museum and studio space. My hope is that there will always be at least one artist living and working there. We live on one side and work in the other, but one day our house can become a cafe and gallery space and transform over time as the needs for the space evolve. It is meant to change its purpose over time."

For now, Kevin and Jennifer Box's original origami sculptures, ranging from small to monumental, enchant and enthrall visitors who make a stop along the Turquoise Trail.

Those who wander the meandering paths of the sculpture garden can closely examine the intricate "folds," which reveal the steps in the process, an appropriate parallel to the process by which the Box studio came to fruition in the Little Garden of the Gods. "What's exciting about origami," says Box, "is that each piece begins with a single uncut piece of paper. For me, that's a great metaphor for life: What we do with that is what defines us."

When back in 2006 the dramatic landscape of a thirty-five-acre property along the Turquoise Trail caught Box's eye, it presented an opportunity. And although the couple's vision for that property is evolving over time, for Kevin Box it has turned out to be one of his most enthralling, exciting, and stimulating artworks. "It's the coolest sculpture I've ever built," he says, "and it's very fun to get to live in your own sculpture."

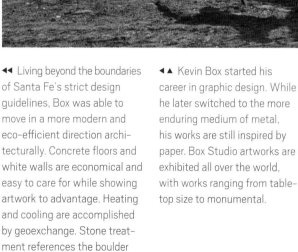

◀◀ Living beyond the boundaries of Santa Fe's strict design guidelines, Box was able to move in a more modern and eco-efficient direction architecturally. Concrete floors and white walls are economical and easy to care for while showing artwork to advantage. Heating and cooling are accomplished by geoexchange. Stone treatment references the boulder garden outside the door.

◀▲ Kevin Box started his career in graphic design. While he later switched to the more enduring medium of metal, his works are still inspired by paper. Box Studio artworks are exhibited all over the world, with works ranging from tabletop size to monumental.

RUSTIC MODERN BARN

When architect John Carney moved to Wyoming in 1992, he left behind a body of work comprised of mostly commercial buildings to relocate to a place where artistic expression would be more personal, a product of synchronicity between architect, client, and setting. Any building designed by Carney in Jackson Hole would combine the architect's knowledge and experience with the clients' aesthetic preferences and programmatic goals. Above all, it would be a response to the land.

Carney was blessed with discerning clients from the start. One of his first commissions was to build a vacation home for a family from Los Angeles. Husband and wife both worked in the film industry and were raising a family in LA, but they needed a respite from both the pace and the milieu of their primary home. The wife had first visited Jackson with her family at age ten, vacationing at Lost Creek Ranch and Jenny Lake Lodge, and the experience had affected her profoundly; her husband, when he discovered Jackson later in life, was equally enthusiastic. It wasn't long before they were under construction on a log home. Fast forward twenty-plus years to a time when the children are grown, retirement is under consideration, and it's now possible to work from anywhere. The owners were already spending half the year in Wyoming and planning to increase that. They explained to Carney (now a longtime friend who in the intervening years had also consulted on their California home), that they envisioned a multiprogram space. It would combine guest quarters, an exercise room, and a workshop for the husband (a hobbyist mechanic) where he could house and tinker with his collection of bicycles, motorcycles, and classic vehicles.

◄◄ Longtime clients of architect John Carney, of Carney Logan Burke Architects, approached him about designing a guest quarters, exercise space, and workshop where the husband could tinker with his bicycles and cars. They envisioned a barn that was traditional in form but modern in attitude.

▲ An art installation of a swarm of butterflies by Paul Villinski, courtesy of Tayloe Piggott Gallery, leads the eye from the entry area up the stairwell to the living space.

◄ Collectible vehicles include a vintage VW bus, perfect for exploring Wyoming's national parks.

The couple wanted a barn, traditional in form but modernized for the twenty-first century. It would be functional, filled with light, and positioned to take advantage of the site's spectacular views. Siting on the mostly level eighteen-acre property was relatively straightforward; it would be close to the main house for convenience and within the allowed building envelope, but offset to the northeast so as not to interfere with the main home's views. The structure is simple in concept: a wood-clad gambrel-roofed barn with small square windows on the lower floor, three pairs of dormer windows, a small cupola, and an attached one-story shed-roofed structure, set back so as not to interfere with the pure lines of the gambrel form. The shed attachment allows for an additional parking bay and lends a feeling of historical authenticity, as barns were often added on to in this way.

The lower floor is the husband's domain, and it was his idea to place large black and white tiles on the floor. These inject animation and a sense of playfulness into the room, while the barn wood walls and sliding doors on rustic hardware lend texture and warmth in the utilitarian space. Bicycles become sculptural when suspended against a wall; a red dune buggy and green-and-white vintage VW van add color.

The upstairs is accessed from its own porch and entryway. In the vestibule a dramatic installation of a Paul Villinski butterfly swarm set against weathered wood leads the eye upstairs to the surprise that awaits. The "aha" moment comes upon reaching the second level. Within the meticulously ordered grid laid out by the articulated beams with steel bracing and dormer windows is an open, airy space with jaw-dropping views through an end wall of floor-to-ceiling windows framing a dramatic outlook of the Tetons.

Two thirds of the upper level is given over to an open plan exercise room, with a kitchenette and sitting/dining area. A walk-through closet, guest bath, and guest bedroom anchor the end of the building closer to the main house. The guest room, viewed from the main house and driveway, has a more traditional window in keeping with the goal of authenticity. "On the south side the barn is much more traditional," explains architect John Carney. The window "looks like it could have been there when

▲ An avid outdoorsman and bicyclist, the husband proposed the idea of installing the large black and white tiles, which brighten, enliven, and lend character to the garage workspace.

▲ The tranquil guest bedroom furnished by Rush Jenkins of WRJ Design relies on luxurious fabrics and multiple textures to create a feeling of comfort. By adhering to a clean palette, he gives voice to the architecture.

hay was being loaded into the loft. You don't know until you go upstairs that the north side is a glass curtain wall."

The interiors were conceived by Rush Jenkins of WRJ Interior Design. "He has such a great eye and was invaluable to me," says the owner. "He led us in a great direction. Contemporary can feel a little stark, but I like it to feel cozy and welcoming."

They attained this feeling of comfort—despite the modernist-leaning furniture and neutral colors—through layers of texture and sumptuous fabrics: a leather and suede headboard on an open frame bed, curtains of Loro Piana linen, impossibly soft throws. Jenkins says that above all his client wanted a clean palette. "The idea was that the architecture and the artwork could be seen," he recalls. "We

talked about it being tone on tone, so it would be about the forms of the furniture, the textures of the fabrics, and the views."

The project was the result of a focus on excellence by John Carney, project architect Matt Bowers, interior designer Rush Jenkins, Benchmark Builder's project foreman Jeff Thomas, and the owners, who brought passion to the project and divvied up their attention to detail by floor and program.

No doubt a career-spanning friendship laid the basis for a productive working relationship. "It's a cool design that was very much a collaboration," says Carney. "I like to think we're encouraging the clients as we go on this trip together."

▲ The quieter end of the barn faces the main house and driveway, giving guests a sense of connection to the action. The immense square window allows plenty of light and adds interest, while the small square window centered above it references traditional barn architecture.

▶ The "aha" moment comes at the top of the stairs when visitors turn and see the floor-to-ceiling glass wall framing the spectacular mountain view. The room is kept deliberately spare in order to appreciate the poetry of the repeating architectural forms.

CREATIVE SPACE FOR A MODERN LIFESTYLE

The story of Jen Perry's writing retreat is a fitting tribute to the romantic ideal of following one's passions, and a testament to the value in finding "a room of one's own." Her in-town apartment, originally conceived as a writing space, office, and occasional crash pad, morphed almost overnight into the bustling headquarters of a start-up outdoor fashion brand. While there's an inherent irony in the fact that a space conceived as a tranquil retreat for one person is now stretched to provide work space for six employees and host a constant stream of meetings, it was precisely *because* Perry had a quiet space (however short-lived that quiet might have been) which allowed her to propel a longtime entrepreneurial idea to a point of resounding success.

Perry was the only female in her household and a busy mom, community contributor, and outdoorswoman when she realized she needed a place where she could pursue her own projects. Specifically, she had a screenplay she wanted to write and she needed an office from which she could help run her family's Montana guest ranch. She found a hidden gem only ten minutes from the just-outside-of-town home she shares with her husband and sons. The apartment was right on Bozeman's main street, above the iconic Burger Bob's. Perry set about transforming the rooms—which had ten-foot-high ceilings and original oak flooring but were in urgent need of refreshing—into a light, airy, and spunkily feminine workplace. It was conceived as a place for quiet inspiration, which would come at least partly from an array of special belongings imbued with

significance, from Perry's collection of Regency romance novels written by her grandmother to memorabilia from her upbringing and travels.

For the small, windowless kitchen, Perry had an idea for cabinets made with antique mirrors. Her search led her to Abby Hetherington, who had just struck out on her own as an independent interior designer. The two found common ground in their creativity and their willingness to push the boundaries of style, so much so that Hetherington ended up doing the interiors for the entire project, then went on to collaborate with Perry in designing her family's modernist main home and playfully western guesthouse. For Hetherington, whose creativity knows no bounds, the project represented an auspicious start to her independent career. "Jen wanted a space that represented her and was a place she could be creative and develop an idea. What's really cool about Jen is that she hired me, but she came up with a lot of ideas. My job was to take her ideas and make them happen."

The former apartment had its limitations, such as a windowless bathroom and kitchen and a narrow hallway, but these were balanced with attributes like high ceilings, large skylights, period details, and a fireplace. The budget allowed for splurges like handmade custom-designed tiles for the kitchen and fireplace surround and a "living wall" of cacti and succulents. These Hetherington offset with creative, cost-effective solutions, such as a mural made from Anthropologie wallpaper, which she separated into sections, hung at different levels, and embellished with upholstery nail heads to create depth and texture. Everything in the apartment has significance, from a seashell chandelier evoking the owner's California childhood to references to New York City, where Perry met her husband. "The house tries to tell her story," explains Hetherington, "but the process was kind of backwards. She would show up with boxes of random stuff and say, 'work it in.' My color palette in the rooms depended on the things she was giving me. These are all things that inspire her and she wanted to be surrounded by them."

Clearly the layers of inspiration yielded results. Perry, who comes from a family of entrepreneurs and business owners, says she had always had the idea for her product but never had the space to

Previous page An in-town work retreat and getaway for a busy mom who lives just outside of Bozeman, Montana, started out as a place to be creative but has adapted to house the headquarters of fit fashion company JeltBelt and its staff of six.

▲ Abby Hetherington designed the interiors, where every item carries significance in Jen Perry's life story. World maps reference places she has traveled, a book-art installation is a tribute to her grandmother, a romance novelist. The white lacquer desk was the client's own. Kirsten Kainz painted the landscape with grazing horses.

► The kitchen has no windows but receives and distributes light from a generous skylight and from cabinets inset with antique mirrors, which Hetherington had made locally. The retro fridge and oven are from Big Chill, the lights from Curry & Company.

◀◀ The living room—eclectic and feminine—juxtaposes a floral skirted ottoman, velvet upholstered armchair, and custom-designed tiles with more rustic nods to nature in the silver-leafed driftwood Arteriors floor lamp and a large living wall of succulents.

◀ White wainscoting creates texture in a monochromatic room and lends an airy cottage feel; the daybed can accommodate overnight visitors.

◄ A narrow hallway is made bigger and brighter with a large mirror. Hetherington crafted the mural-like wall treatment from decorative paper panels purchased at Anthropologie, which she embellished with upholstery nail heads for depth and texture. The phone bench, sourced through 1st Dibs, was painted black and re-covered in a Rose Cumming fabric. The vintage chandelier was found at a local antique shop.

▶ A foyer area is furnished to be versatile; the tall bistro table and velvet upholstered stools can be moved out of the way for a party or business gathering. The Noir light fixture and a faux crocodile wall covering from Osborne & Little add texture and interest.

work through the process of having it prototyped, patented, and sold. An outdoor enthusiast, Perry explains, "I had been thinking of an elastic belt with a low-profile buckle that I could wear with my skinny jeans or ski pants. I always wanted to launch an invention and having a creative place to myself allowed that to happen. Now we call my office Jelt Headquarters."

Jelt is an innovative company whose main product is a versatile belt that can transition with ease from ski slopes through airports and to the boardroom. Launched from Perry's office in 2014, the belt is highly functional, sustainably made (100 percent from water bottles), Montana crafted (by incarcerated women), and philanthropically minded. With several full time employees, plus a couple of part-time

employees, the quiet writing retreat has had to adapt.

Perry removed a lot of personal photos and objects in order to make room for printers, computers, and chairs; she rearranged furniture to accommodate more people and desks. "As far as the transformation from 'a room of one's own' to Jelt Headquarters, I have come a long way," she says. But it's worth it: "It might be the coolest office ever. People who come by for meetings are always impressed and never want to leave."

The space has proven versatile; perhaps it will transform again in the future. Perry might still pursue writing. After all, she points out, her grandmother published twenty-seven romance novels *after* she retired.

ART & WELLNESS AT LAKE'S EDGE

Whitefish Lake has a well-deserved reputation as a vacation paradise. The seven-mile-long, mountain-rimmed lake—with its world-class ski mountain, extensive national forest lands, and immediate access to Glacier National Park—beckons outdoor enthusiasts in all seasons. Its natural beauty and outdoor recreation opportunities are limitless. For those who call it home, however, it is truly remote. And located just fifty miles south of the Canadian border, Whitefish can have long, dark winters.

Longtime residents, a husband and wife with grown children, had no intention of giving up their home to retreat to warmer climes, as so many do upon retirement. Instead, they came up with a creative solution to combat cabin fever and winter chills, one that allows them to make the most of their spectacular setting in all seasons while offering a way to stay warm, physically fit, aesthetically nourished, and bathed in light on even the darkest days.

Their property, a steep, wooded peninsula that juts into the lake at its northwest corner, had housed the family home for decades. The clients loved their home and had no interest in changing its traditional construction or footprint. But there was a dilapidated guesthouse on the property that had outlived its usefulness yet commanded a valuable vantage point over the sparkling waters of the lake. With the help of David Koel of CTA Architects, Susie Hoffmann of Envi Design, and the clients' architecturally trained son, the couple envisioned a new structure that would support their long-term wellness on a variety of levels. It would be a multipurpose, multilevel building whose modernist design would both stand out and fit into the landscape, while creating a vibrant, dynamic contrast to the existing residence.

The building was to house a serene spa with a walk-through shower and Japanese-style soaking tub, a workout facility, a lap pool, and a formal art gallery designed to showcase the owners' collection of Asian art. It may seem like an amalgamation of disparate functions; the relationship lies in the fact that each function promotes wellness. This is a particular focus of Envi Design's Susie Hoffmann, and an important long-term consideration for the clients, given the extreme climatic conditions found in northern Montana.

The design was conceived as two pitch-roofed forms with a rectangular glass extrusion to add dynamic tension and interest. The steep pitch of the slope, the trees, and the green roof of the glassed-in lap pool serve to blend the structure into the landscape, affording it spectacular views of the lake and surrounding mountains while minimizing its presence.

The three connected units allow for both subtlety and surprise. The vertical structures hug the hillside and nestle into existing trees, while the flat-roofed, glass-enclosed lap pool, set at an angle to the anchoring elements, protrudes out of the hillside. From the exterior, "it defies the site in a contrast to nature, because it pushes against the contours of the hill at an angle," says the architect. "From the inside, though, it's the reverse. Because of all the glass, you feel as though you're in the treetops." The overall effect is ethereal. "It perches way up on a hillside and seems to defy gravity," adds Koel. "It hovers there."

The complex has two approaches. The more formal approach for visitors has a long, gently sloping walkway of irregularly cut slate leading to a glass entry flanked by the two vertical forms; there is a more private path on the other side for the residents. The entry opens to a soothing palette of cream and

▲ A secondary structure built for a couple who live full time in northern Montana is all about wellness, both physical and aesthetic. The combination fitness center, spa, and fine art gallery was designed by architect David Koel of CTA with Susie Hoffmann of Envi Design and with input from the owners' son.

▶ A walk-through shower leads to a Japanese soaking tub overlooking a tranquil rock garden.

◄◄ The lap pool is ever conscious of its relationship to the lake. The waters are visible through the trees from the pool; teak decking speaks to docks at lake's edge. Susie Hoffmann designed the lines of inset lights to serve as guides so that swimmers doing the back-stroke would know when they were approaching the end of the lane.

◄ At the entry, the gallery lies in one direction, a seating area with mod furniture and the pool in the other. Stairs lead to the workout room/yoga studio and rooftop terrace.

▼ The wood-clad room housing the Japanese bath has an ethereal calm with its quiet prospect, infinity-edge tub, and floating bench.

gray, which promotes a feeling of serenity in a space filled with soft natural light. To one side, at the base of the stairs leading to the exercise facility, there's a sitting area at the end of the lap pool, which is partially surrounded by teak flooring. The teak planks give the feel of an extremely refined dock, thereby linking the experience to the lake outside the window. To the other side is a small jewel of an art gallery, accessed by a large custom-made glass door which pivots closed to protect the art from the pool's humidity. The room is well lit and highly finished, with pedestals and shelves for pottery, ceramics, textiles, and a large, multipanel screen. Minimal, offset windows allow greater wall space for hanging flat art.

On the hill-hugging side of the structure, a walk-through shower leads to the soaking tub room, a tranquil space with views of the lake but oriented toward a Japanese-style garden whose granite boulders and sculptural native vegetation nestle into the hillside. "The concept was to make it a more introspective space," explains Koel. "Rather than overlooking the big panorama of the lake, your focus is up close, on the textures and colors found within the landscaped hillside. It's two very different experiences."

▲ Shoji screens carry the Japanese aesthetic into the bathroom.

▶ A light-filled workout room overlooks the lake and a living roof.

Susie Hoffmann, who has an extensive background in wellness design, envisioned a floating bench made from partially petrified wood imported from Thailand and a raised infinity-edge bath that can be afforded privacy with movable Shoji screens. The clients, she says, "were very clear that they wanted it to feel like a Japanese bathhouse. They embraced the concepts and elements of that design. We had an understanding of what the experience should be, and that, rather than just the aesthetics, led the design."

An exercise room, small kitchen, powder room, and changing room complete the interior spaces, with mechanical needs (extensive, because of humidity management) housed out of sight. The group worked to keep transitions smooth, from room to room, from indoor to out. Concrete interior walls create a homogeneous feel. Double-wide exterior sliding doors disappear to blur the transition between indoor and out. A large green roof and patio area with chaise lounges offer outdoor opportunities and open the structure to the lake and surrounding forest.

What's unusual about the outcome, beyond the unique combination of programs under one roof, is the warmth and livability achieved within the minimalist aesthetic. Hoffmann says they created a unified, harmonious whole by employing a limited palette of colors, plaster, wood, stone, and glass but using changes in texture and plane to create vibrancy and interest. They also used local materials (quarried black limestone from Roundup, Montana, for example) whenever possible. The modern, clean-line elements meant there would be no molding or trim to hide rough edges or cover up imperfections. There would be forms and planes, but no unnecessary articulation. "The idea," she explains, "was to keep it minimal so that the program of each room could speak for itself."

"We wanted every wall to be a perfect expression of material," adds Koel. This approach necessitated the highest level of craftsmanship and the most meticulous attention to detail. The spot where a built-in bench intersected with a wall, for instance, was very specific, very thought through. "We all had the same philosophy of minimalism," he explains. "*Simplicity* was a term that was used a lot. Simplicity is hard. You'd think simplicity would be easy to achieve, but what it requires is a tremendous amount of design

restraint. Simplicity is a challenge, but when you achieve it, it shimmers."

The project owes its success to a harmonious collaboration between the design professionals and the family, and the fact that all agreed not to hurry or force the process. In fact, the project took three years, a long time for an ancillary structure. Architect and designer spent a lot of time together, as well as with the clients and their son, who was very active in the design and collaboration.

"Sometimes this can have a stifling effect," concedes Koel, "but he was really active and became an integral part of the design team. It's kind of rare that at some point you don't know whose idea was whose but you work as a unified team to make it beautiful. We were designing together for the greater good."

In the end, says, Koel, "It was fun to work with clients who had the interest and patience to let us work through the ideas. Most clients at some point just want it done. These wanted it to be done right."

◄ A one-room art gallery was designed specifically for the owners' art collection. Many of the pieces were acquired on trips to Asia.

▲ The long, narrow lap pool structure juts out from the main structure, providing the perfect place to appreciate the natural beauty of the lake and forest.

RUSTIC MODERN RESOURCES

ARCHITECTURE, DESIGN & CONSTRUCTION

Architect's Wife
www.architectswife.com

Benchmark Builders
www.benchmarkjh.com

Tracey Byrne, The
Waldyn Group
tracey@waldyngroup.com

Carney Logan Burke Architects
and Interior Design
www.clbarchitects.com

Catherine Lane Interiors
Livingston, MT

CTA Architects, David Koel
www.ctagroup.com

David Naylor Interiors
www.davidnaylorinteriors.com

Dembergh Construction
www.demberghjh.com

Denman Construction
www.denmanconstruction.com

Dressel Construction
www.dresselco.com

Envi Interior Design Studio
www.envidesign.com

Fletcher & Hardoin Architects,
Dan Fletcher
www.fletcherhardoin.com

Frank Lloyd Wright School
of Architecture
www.taliesin.edu

Hensel Design Studios
www.henseldesignstudios.com

Abby Hetherington
www.abbyhetheringtoninte-
riors.com

JLF Design Build
www.jlfdesignbuild.com

Arnelle Kase
arnellekase@gmail.com

Kevin Box Studio
www.outsidetheboxstudio.com

Laura Fedro Interiors
www.laurafedrointeriors.com

Linda Lamb
www.lambdesigngroup.com

Locati Architects
www.locatiarchitects.com

Lohss Construction
www.lohssconstruction.com

Martel Construction
www.martelconstruction.com

Maya Design Studio
www.studio-maya.com

Patno Construction
Jackson, Wyoming

Pearson Design Group
www.pearsondesigngroup.com

Reid Smith Architects
www.reidsmitharchitects.com

Sandmeyer Design
www.sandmeyerdesign.com

Schlauch Bottcher
Construction
www.sbconstruction.com

Stocker & Allaire General
Contractors
www.stockerallaire.com

Tayloe Piggot
www.tayloepiggottgallery.com

Tom Ochsner Architect
www.tomochsnerarchitect.com

Urbaine Home
www.urbainehome.com

WRJ Design
www.wrjdesign.com

ABOUT THE AUTHOR

Chase Reynolds Ewald has been writing about food, design, travel, and lifestyle in the West and beyond for 25 years. A graduate of Yale and the Graduate School of Journalism at U.C. Berkeley, she is a contributing editor of *Western Art & Architecture Magazine.* This is her ninth book and her fourth collaboration with Audrey Hall.

ABOUT THE PHOTOGRAPHER

Audrey Hall's images about culture, style, and travel are diversely featured, from social media campaigns to television. She was recently on the road in Africa, Haiti, and domestically with Pulitzer Prize–winning journalist Nicholas Kristof for the PBS series *A Path Appears.* This is her eleventh book.